The Blue Book of Canadian Cuisine

A Tribute to
Elected Progressive Conservative Members
and Senators
and a Galaxy of Good Eating

Compiled and Coordinated
by
Eunice Taylor

Front cover photograph — Steamed Blueberry Pudding, page 172

The Blue Book of Canadian Cuisine
by
Eunice Taylor

First Printing — September, 1985
Copyright © 1985 by
Annaperce Holdings Ltd.
Box 606
Melfort, Saskatchewan
Canada   S0E 1A0

Canadian Cataloguing in Publication Data

Main entry under title:

The Blue Book of Canadian Cuisine

Includes index.
ISBN 0-919845-33-9

1. Cookery, Canadian. I. Taylor, Eunice, 1929-
TX715.B598 1985   641.5971   C85-091431-0

Front Cover Photograph by
Patricia Holdsworth
Patricia Holdsworth Photography
Regina, Saskatchewan

Designed, Printed and Produced in Canada by
Centax of Canada
Publishing Consultant and Food Stylist: Margo Embury
Designer: Blair Fraser

1048 Fleury Street
Regina, Saskatchewan, Canada S4N 4W8
(306) 359-3737

#105-4711 13 Street N.E.
Calgary, Alberta, Canada T2E 6M3

Table of Contents

Introduction

September 1984 saw the election of the largest Progressive Conservative government majority in the history of Canada. To celebrate this historic event, plus the preponderance of elected provincial Progressive Conservative members across Canada, my husband, Lyle, and I were inspired to publish "The Blue Book of Canadian Cuisine". This cookbook, a collection of treasured family recipes from Conservative members and senators coast to coast, was designed as a tribute. It has also emerged as an accurate reflection of the wonderful regional and ethnic diversity of Canadian cuisine.

Thank you to all who responded to my request for recipes, your enthusiastic response, support and good wishes are greatly appreciated.

I wish to particularly acknowledge the generous assistance and efforts of Jack Scowen, M.P., Grant Hodgins, M.L.A., Carol McKerracher, Marie Letcher, Bunny Scowen and Senator Martha Bielish.

Eunice Taylor

Eunice Taylor

Message from Premier Grant Devine

As leader of the Progressive Conservative Party and Premier of the Province of Saskatchewan, it gives me great pleasure to extend my congratulations on the production of this Progressive Conservative cookbook.

This recipe collection provides us with a unique view of the men and women who have run for office, served us so well and continue to serve us today. It is a refreshing chance for a glimpse into the personalities of these Progressive Conservatives, not to mention an opportunity to sample some delicious food.

I commend all those involved in producing and contributing to this collection. To all readers, I extend best wishes for good cooking and great eating!

Yours sincerely,

Grant Devine

Grant Devine
Premier

Appetizers and Beverages

Cocktail Crisps

1 cup	butter	⅛-¼ tsp.	each cayenne, pepper and
8 oz. pkg.	Imperial cheese		Tabasco
¼ tsp.	salt	4 cups	Rice Krispies cereal
1½ cups	flour		

Soften butter and cream cheese, mix together, add salt, stir in flour, add peppers, Tabasco and Rice Krispies. Mix well, shape in small balls and press down with a fork. Place on an unbuttered baking sheet.

Bake at 350°F for 15 to 20 minutes or until lightly brown.

Makes about 2 dozen. Serve cold or warm.

Guy and Yolande Charbonneau
Hon. Guy Charbonneau
(Speaker-Président)
The Senate
Québec

Pâté de Poulet

Couper le poulet et/ou la dinde en dés et mesurer. Pour chaque tasse de poulet ajouter une tasse de chacun des ingrédients suivant:

carottes	oignons
céléri	navet
patates	

Mettre dans un chaudron et couvrir de bouillon de poulet. Assaisonner de sel et poivre au goût. Ajouter ½ tasse de Bovril aux légumes. Faire cuire jusqu'à ce que les légumes soient mi-cuits.

Epaissir avec du Bistro.

Remplir le fond de tarte et couvrir d'une abaisse. DELICIEUX.

Lise Bourgault, M.P.
Argenteuil-Papineau
Québec

Salmon Pâté

10 oz.	can tomato soup	7¾ oz.	can red salmon, boned
¾	soup can of water		juice of ½ lemon
4 oz.	pkg. pimiento cream cheese	2 pkg.	unflavoured gelatin
1	small onion, minced	1 cup	mayonnaise

Heat together first 4 ingredients, then stir in next 3 until gelatin is dissolved. Cool. Stir in mayonnaise. Oil loaf tin or mould, pour in mixture and refrigerate. Unmould and serve with sour cream and fresh dill.

Shirley and David Crombie
Hon. David Crombie, M.P.
Rosedale
Ontario

Antipasto

3 x 6.5 oz.	cans whole tuna and oil	12 oz.	jar gherkins
14 oz.	bottle ketchup	2 x 10 oz.	cans mushrooms
16 oz.	bottle chili sauce	4 oz.	can smoked oysters or clams
12 oz.	jar olives		juice of 2 lemons
12 oz.	jar pickled onions.		

Put in large bowl and mix by hand until well mixed. Spoon into sealers. Makes approximately 2½ quarts. Keeps well in refrigerator.

John and Lise Gormley
John Gormley, M.P.
The Battlefords-Meadow Lake
Saskatchewan

Antipasto

2 lbs.	cauliflower	1	tin black olives
2 lbs.	pickling onions	5 x 10 oz.	tins mushrooms
2 lbs.	dill pickles (2 qts.)	2 x 7½ oz.	tins tuna fish
2 x 14 oz.	tins green beans, drained	1	large tin anchovies
2 x 14 oz.	tins yellow beans, drained	4	large bottles ketchup
2 lbs.	green peppers	1½ cups	vinegar
2 lbs.	red peppers	1½ cups	mazola oil
1	large jar green olives		

Cut up all the vegetables into small pieces. Add to all the other ingredients, except the anchovies and tuna. Boil 15 minutes, then add the fish. Cook another 5 minutes.

Put into jars. Seal and process in a canner for 20-30 minutes.

James and Betty Horsman
Hon. James Horsman, M.L.A.
Medicine Hat
Alberta

Shrimp Mould or Dip

10 oz.	can tomato soup	1 cup	chopped celery
1 cup	mayonnaise	¼ cup	chopped onion
1	envelope unflavoured gelatin	2 x 4 oz.	cans small shrimp pieces,
8 oz.	cream cheese, softened		rinsed and coarsely
	(125 g)		chopped

Heat soup with gelatin until warm.

Remove from stove, add rest of ingredients and stir with mixer.

Pour into 1 or 2 greased moulds, at least 24 hours before needed, or put into crock or dip pot.

Serve with Sociables crackers.

Bob and Joan Hicks
Bob Hicks, M.P.
Scarborough East
Ontario

Shrimp Dip

½ cup	chili sauce	2 tbsp.	fresh horseradish
½ cup	ketchup	1 tsp.	paprika
2 tbsp.	Worcestershire sauce	2 x 4 oz.	cans shrimp, drained and washed
2 tbsp.	prepared mustard		

Combine all ingredients and chill for several hours to blend flavours.

Bob Jackson, M.L.A.
St. Stephen-Campobello
New Brunswick

Seafood Mousse

This appetizing mould is popular in at least two conservative households.

10 oz.	cream of mushroom soup	½ cup	chopped green onions
6 oz.	cream cheese	1 cup	mayonnaise
1	envelope gelatin	5 oz.	tin crab meat
½ cup	cold water	¼ tsp.	curry powder
½ cup	finely chopped celery		

Heat soup and cheese until melted and smooth. Soften gelatin in water, sprinkle over water in a small bowl, for 5 mintues. Add gelatin to soup mixture. Then add remaining ingredients. Mix well. Pour into oiled 1-quart mould overnight.
NOTE: This may be served with crackers as an appetizer spread or as a luncheon salad.

John, Cate, Sheena, Anna and Mary Fraser
Hon. John A. Fraser, P.C., Q.C., M.P.
Vancouver South
British Columbia
and
Bob Pickering, M.L.A.
Bengough - Milestone
Saskatchewan

Great Aunt Blanche's Cheese Ball

8 oz.	tub Imperial cheese		1 tsp.	Lee and Perrins
1 lb.	Philadelphia cream cheese			Worcestershire sauce
4 oz.	Danish blue cheese		2-3	drops Tabasco
	garlic salt, 2 or 3 shakes			walnuts or parsley

Let cheeses soften and mix until well blended. Add garlic salt, Worcestershire sauce and Tabasco. Roll in large ball or several smaller ones (It is easier to form into balls if chilled first). Roll balls in finely chopped walnuts or parsley. Wrap in plastic wrap and then in foil. These freeze well and can be refrozen.

Hon. Fred Bradley, M.L.A.
Pincher Creek/Crowsnest
Alberta

Chip Dip

3 cups	Hellman's mayonnaise		1½ tsp.	Worcestershire sauce
1½ cups	sour cream		¾ tsp.	paprika
1½ tbsp.	lemon juice		⅜ tsp.	curry powder
3 tbsp.	onion flakes, or dry onion soup			salt
¼ cup	dry parsley			

Combine all ingredients. Mix well and refrigerate for several hours to blend flavours.

Hon. Wilfred G. Bishop, M.L.A.
Queens North
New Brunswick

Cheese Log

½ lb.	medium Cheddar cheese	1 tsp.	grated onion
4 oz.	cream cheese	1½ tsp.	Worcestershire sauce
4 oz.	pimiento cheese	1 tsp.	lemon juice
1 tsp.	salt		pecans or parsley
⅛ tsp.	pepper		

Grate Cheddar cheese and mix with remaining ingredients. Roll in shape of a log, in waxed paper, then unwrap and roll log in ground pecans or parsley. Store in refrigerator.

Ronald A. Stewart, M.P.
Simcoe South
Ontario

Tuna Ball

6.5 oz.	can tuna	1 tbsp.	finely chopped onion
1 tbsp.	lemon juice	½ tsp.	Tabasco
2 tsp.	horseradish	½ cup	chopped pecans
¼ tsp.	Worcestershire sauce	3 tbsp.	finely chopped parsley
8 oz.	pkg. cream cheese, softened		

Combine first 7 ingredients and chill. Shape into a ball. Roll in nuts and parsley. Serve with crackers.

H. Neil Windsor, P. Eng., M.H.A.
Mount Pearl
Newfoundland

Artichoke Delight

14 oz.	can unpickled artichoke hearts	Parmesan cheese, to taste
3 tbsp.	mayonnaise	Melba toast

Drain artichoke hearts. Cut each into quarters. In a small bowl, mix well mayonnaise with grated Parmesan cheese according to personal taste. Mixture should be fairly thick. Place ¼ artichoke heart on Melba toast round or on any small firm cracker. Add a lump of mayonnaise/cheese mixture, approximately 1 teaspoon. Bake at 350°F for 10 to 15 minutes. Finish by broiling for 1 minute.

Bob and Lorraine Pennock
Bob Pennock, M.P.
Etobicoke North
Ontario

Deep-Fried Fish

1½ cups	flour	¾ cup	flat beer
1 tsp.	melted butter	2	egg whites, beaten
2	egg yolks, beaten		

Combine first 4 ingredients and let rest in refrigerator 3-12 hours. Add 2 egg whites immediately before using. Cut fish fillets into bite-sized pieces. (Almost any kind of fish will do — tastes best if you caught it yourself). Dip in batter and then put into hot oil in a deep-fryer. Fish is ready when it floats to the top.
Serve with melted crab apple jelly for dipping.

Rick Swenson, M.L.A.
Thunder Creek
Saskatchewan

Chicken Wings in Garlic Soy Sauce (Lee Yeow Kai Yik)

1 lb.	chicken wings	1 tbsp.	cooking oil
	honey or corn syrup,	½ tsp.	finely chopped ginger root
1-1½ tbsp.	OR 1½ tbsp. sugar		OR ¼ tsp. ginger powder
	dark soy sauce	¼ tsp.	minced garlic
1-1½ tbsp.	salt pepper to taste	½ tsp.	finely chopped onion

Wash and dry chicken wings. Disjoint into small pieces and put into a deep casserole dish or mixing bowl. Add honey, soy sauce, salt and pepper to taste and mix thoroughly. Marinate overnight preferably, otherwise stand at least for 30 minutes.

Put cooking oil into frying pan. Add ginger, garlic and onion when oil is smoking hot. Brown slightly and add chicken pieces, saving the marinade. Fry the chicken pieces, turning over until light brown, using maximum heat. Lower heat to medium and continue cooking for 20-30 minutes, turning chicken wings over occasionally. When cooked, place in serving dish on a bed of lettuce or sliced cucumber after draining off the excess oil. Put the marinade into the frying pan. Add ½ cup of water and bring to a boil rapidly. Thicken sauce as desired, using cornstarch, and pour over the chicken pieces. Decorate with sprigs of parsley, spring onions or celery leaves. Serves 2.

NOTE: For a smoky taste flame chicken with 2 tbsp. brandy then add sauce.

Donald Stewart, M.H.A.
Fortune-Hermitage
Newfoundland and Labrador

Chicken Wings

12-15	chicken wings	½ cup	butter or margarine
1 cup	soy sauce	1 tsp.	dry mustard
1 cup	packed brown sugar	¾ cup	water

Break off boney tip of chicken wings and discard. Combine soy sauce, brown sugar, butter, dry mustard and water in saucepan and heat, stirring until all ingredients have dissolved. Marinate chicken wings at least 2 hours in sauce, turning occasionally. Arrange on baking sheet; bake at 350°F for 45 minutes. Drain on paper towels. Serve hot or cold.

Vince Dantzer, M.P.
Okanagan North
British Columbia

Chinese Chicken Wings

Provide a good supply of napkins or finger bowls for your guests when serving these flavourful wings.

3½ lb.	chicken wings (about 20)	1	garlic clove, minced
¼ cup	granulated sugar	⅔ cup	ketchup
1 tsp.	salt	½ cup	soy sauce
¾ tsp.	ginger	¼ cup	dry red wine

Cut chicken wings into 3 pieces by cutting at joints. Discard tips or reserve for soup. In 13" x 9" baking dish, arrange chicken in single layer. Mix remaining ingredients and pour over chicken. Cover and refrigerate overnight, stirring occasionally.

Drain chicken, reserving marinade. Place chicken on foil-lined baking sheet. Brush with marinade and bake in 375°F oven for 40-50 minutes or until tender, basting occasionally. Remove immediately from foil to serving platter and serve hot. Makes about 40 appetizers.

Hon. Mary J. LeMessurier, M.L.A.
Edmonton Centre
Alberta

Japanese Chicken Wings

3 lbs.	chicken wings	3 tbsp.	water
1	egg, beaten	1 cup	white sugar
1 cup	flour	½ cup	vinegar
1 cup	butter	1 tsp.	Accent
3 tbsp.	soy sauce	½ tsp.	salt

Cut wings in half. Dip in slightly beaten egg and then in flour. Fry in butter until deep brown and crisp. Put in shallow raosting pan. Combine remaining ingredients to make sauce and pour sauce over wings.

Bake at 350°F for ½ hour. Spoon sauce over wings during cooking. Great for crowds, kids and snacks. These taste good warmed up if there are any left over and they are also great cold. Freezes well.

Russ Sutor, M.L.A.
Regina North East
Saskatchewan

Appetizer Turnovers

Pastry:

1 cup	cold butter	8 oz.	cream cheese (500 g)
2 cups	flour		

Cut butter into flour until crumbly. Cut in cream, then gather dough into a ball. Divide into 4, wrap well, refrigerate overnight or a few hours. Roll dough into thin circles, cut into 2" circles. Reroll extra dough and cut. Makes 6-7 dozen. Fill and bake.

Turnovers can be made in advance and frozen. Reheat 12 minutes if frozen or 10 minutes if thawed, at 400°F, or microwave on high 4-5 minutes depending on quantity and if frozen or thawed.

Mexican Turnover Filling:

¾ cup	Cheddar or Monterey Jack cheese	1 tsp.	oregano
		2 tsp.	chili powder
¼ cup	black pitted olives	1	small onion, finely chopped
1½ tbsp.	finely chopped Jalapēno (hot) peppers	1	clove garlic, minced
		½ tsp.	cumin

Mix filling ingredients together. Place 1 tsp. on each pastry circle. Fold pastry over and seal with egg white. Place on greased cookie sheet. Prick each with fork to allow steam to escape. If desired, brush with egg/cream glaze (1 egg mixed with 1 tbsp. cream) before baking. Bake in preheated 375°F oven 20 minutes. Makes 3-4 dozen turnovers.

Mushroom Turnover Filling:

2 cups	finely chopped mushrooms	½ tsp.	thyme
½ cup	finely chopped onion	2 tbsp.	flour
¼ cup	butter	2 tbsp.	milk
1 tsp.	salt	1	egg, beaten

Sauté mushrooms and onion in butter until onion is transparent. Stir in salt, thyme, flour and milk. Place 1 tbsp. filling on each pastry circle. Seal edges with milk and egg mixture. Place on cookie sheet and bake at 400°F for 12 minutes until golden brown. 4-5 dozen turnovers.

Myles and Marilyn Morin
Myles Morin, M.L.A.
Battlefords
Saskatchewan

Potato Skins

My favorite snack to serve at parties.

potatoes	bacon bits
melted butter	sour cream
grated cheese	

Choose medium to small potatoes. Bake for 1 hour at 375°F. Slice in half and scoop out potato to within ⅛" of the outer skin. Baste inside and out with melted butter. Place in oven for 7 to 8 minutes at 375°F. Remove and fill with choice of grated cheese and bacon bits, either real or simulated. When ready to serve, place in oven at 375°F until cheese melts. Serve with sour cream.

Dennis H. Cochrane, M.P.
Moncton
New Brunswick

Milt Pahl's Eskimo Wine

1 lb.   green seedless grapes

Wash and drain dry green seedless grapes. Place in freezer on a plate. Serve frozen for a cooling snack on a hot day.

Hon. Milt Pahl, M.L.A.
Edmonton-Mill Woods
Alberta

Miramichi Slush

4	tea bags	12 oz.	frozen lemonade concentrate
2 cups	boiling water	12 oz.	unsweetened orange juice
7 cups	water (5 cups plus ice cubes)		concentrate
		40 oz.	vodka
2 cups	white sugar		7-Up

Steep tea in boiling water, then remove tea bags. Add tea to ice water and juice concentrates. Bring to boil, then cool. Add vodka and freeze for 48 hours. Serve with 7-Up and straws.

Bud Jardine, M.P.
Northumberland-Miramichi
New Brunswick

Tropical Slush

4 cups	white sugar		juice of 2 oranges
6 cups	water	48 oz.	unsweetened pineapple juice
2-3	bananas, blended	12 oz.	lemon juice (real lemon)
	juice of 2 lemons	26 oz.	vodka or white rum

Boil sugar and water 15 minutes. Cool 15 minutes. (You could reduce sugar, as this is pretty sweet).

Mix all in large bowl. Freeze 48 hours. Mix once. To serve, mix half and half, or to taste with 7-Up, Sprite or ginger ale.

Keep in freezer.

Gordon and Shirley Currie
Hon. Gordon Currie, M.L.A.
Regina Wascana
Saskatchewan

Lemonade Base

6 cups	sugar		rind of 4 lemons
2 oz.	citric acid		juice of 6 lemons
1 oz.	tartaric acid	6 cups	boiling water.

Combine all ingredients. Stir until dissolved. Use 1 part base to 5 parts water.

Don and Marg Ravis
Don Ravis, M.P.
Saskatoon East
Saskatchewan

Mulled Wine

For a 1 litre bottle of wine:

1½ cups	water	2	cinnamon sticks
4	whole cloves		grated rind of ¼ lemon
3-4	whole allspice		honey, optional

For 6, 1 litre bottles:

9 cups	water	12	cinnamon sticks
24	whole cloves		grated rind of 1½ lemons
22	whole allspice		honey*

Boil ingredients, (but not the wine) for 15 minutes, stirring occasionally. Do not cover. You could use a little more allspice and cinnamon if desired. Strain and bottle.

To serve, heat spiced mixture almost to boiling. Heat red wine, but do not boil, and add to spices. Serve hot.

*For 6 bottles of mulled wine, I add about 1½ lbs. of honey, for a richer taste.

Geoff Scott, M.P.
Hamilton-Wentworth
Ontario.

Brunches, Lunches and Breads

Florentine Crêpe Cups

1½ cups	shredded Cheddar cheese (6 oz.)	4 oz.	can mushrooms, drained salt and pepper
3 tbsp.	flour	12	prepared crêpes (recipe follows)
3	eggs		
⅔ cup	mayonnaise		
10 oz.	frozen chopped spinach, thawed and drained		

Toss cheese with flour. Add remaining ingredients. Mix well. Fit crêpes into greased muffin pans. Fill with cheese mixture. Bake at 350°F for 40 minutes. Garnish with bacon curls. Makes enough for 12 crêpes.

Basic Crêpe Batter

1 cup	flour	½ cup	water
2	eggs	¼ tsp.	salt
½ cup	milk	2 tbsp.	melted butter

Blend all ingredients thoroughly. Cook briefly on each side in crêpe pan, until lightly browned. Enough for 12 crêpes.

Tim and Fran Embury
Hon. T. B. Embury, M.L.A.
Regina Lakeview
Saskatchewan

Baked Cheese and Tomato Pie

A pie without crust, flavoured tomatoes are topped with a cheese custard. It is equally good hot or cold, an excellent summer lunch.

1 cup	fine fresh breadcrumbs	¼ tsp.	pepper
2 tbsp.	soft butter or margarine	2	green onions, finely chopped
2 tbsp.	grated Swiss cheese	1 tbsp.	butter
2	large OR 4 medium firm ripe tomatoes	2	eggs, lightly beaten
		1 cup	light cream or milk
½ tsp.	honey or sugar	½ cup	grated Swiss or Gouda cheese
½ tsp.	salt		
½ tsp.	basil		salt and pepper

Make the crust by stirring together with your fingers the breadcrumbs, 2 tablespoons soft butter, and the 2 tablespoons grated Swiss cheese. Pat in the bottom of an 8" or 9" pie plate. Bake in a 400°F oven for 10 minutes or until lightly browned. Cool on cake rack.

When crust has cooled, slice unpeeled or peeled tomatoes, place in layers on the crust, sprinkle with sugar or honey, salt, basil, pepper and green onions. Dot with butter.

Beat together the eggs, cream or milk, and grated Swiss or Gouda cheese. Season with salt and pepper to taste. Pour over tomatoes. Bake in a 375°F oven for 30 to 40 minutes or until custard has set. Serves 6.

Jim and Joanne Hawkes
Jim Hawkes, M.P.
Calgary West
Alberta

Spinach Pie

¼ cup	margarine or butter, melted	16 oz.	2% creamed cottage cheese
1¼ cups	fine bread crumbs	2 tbsp.	or to taste, grated cheese
2 tbsp.	cheese, or to taste (old Cheddar, Parmesan or mozzarella)		(old Cheddar, Parmesan or mozzarella)
		2 tbsp.	flour
10 oz.	pkg. frozen chopped spinach, defrosted, water squeezed out		salt and pepper to taste
		2	eggs

Mix first 3 ingredients and line 9" pie plate with ¾ of mixture. Mix remaining ingredients, put in pie shell, and sprinkle remainder of crumbs on top. Bake at 350°F for 40 minutes. Cuts as easily as any pie. Serve with a salad.

Duff and Mary Roblin
Hon. D. Roblin
Government Leader
The Senate
Manitoba

Spinach Tart

3 x 10 oz.	pkg. frozen spinach	3	egg yolks*
	OR	¾ cup	light cream*
2	bunches fresh spinach		salt, pepper to taste
1	small onion, minced	pinch	nutmeg
2 tbsp.	butter	3 tbsp.	grated Parmesan cheese

Cook and drain the spinach. Sauté onion in butter until it is transparent. Mix egg yolks and cream. Add seasonings and cheese. Mix everything together in greased shallow casserole. Bake at 350°F for 15 minutes. This can be prepared a day in advance and refrigerated. Just bake a little longer. Serves 4-6.
*Instead of egg yolks and light cream, you can use 2 eggs and evaporated milk or even ⅔ cup 2% milk.

Doug and Linda Lewis
Doug Lewis, M.P.
Simcoe North
Ontario

Zucchini Pie

This makes a delicious luncheon dish.

	pie crust or Pillsbury Crescent Rolls	½ tsp.	pepper
4 cups	thinly sliced zucchini	¼ tsp.	garlic powder
1 cup	chopped onion	¼ tsp.	basil
¼-½ cup	margarine	¼ tsp.	oregano
½ cup	chopped parsley	2	eggs, beaten
½ tsp.	salt	8 oz.	mozzarella cheese
		2 tsp.	French's mustard

Line a pie plate with pastry or rolls. The rolls are nicest. Flatten them and line the pie plate bottom and the edges. Cook zucchini and onion in margarine for 10 minutes. Add herbs and spices. Combine this with eggs and cheese. Spread pie crust with mustard. Pour in vegetable mixture and then bake at 375°F for 20 minutes or until done.

Hon. George Hees, P.C., M.P.
Northumberland
Ontario

Luncheon Pie

3 tbsp.	butter	2 tbsp.	chopped celery
3 tbsp.	flour	2 tbsp.	chopped onion
2 cups	milk	2	eggs, separated
1 cup	grated sharp cheese	dash	Worcestershire sauce
2 x 6.5 oz.	cans tuna	10"	uncooked pie shell

Make cheese sauce with first 4 ingredients. Remove ½ cup of sauce and set aside. Combine rest of sauce with other ingredients except egg whites and place mixture in pie shell.

Bake 30 minutes at 350°F.

Meanwhile, beat egg whites until stiff then fold in remaining sauce. Place on top of pie. Return to oven until browned.

Hon. John M. Turner, M.P.P.
Peterborough
Ontario

Broccoli-Mushroom-Noodle Casserole

2	stalks fresh broccoli	3	large eggs
1 lb.	fresh mushrooms	3 cups	cottage or ricotta cheese
1	large onion	1½ cups	sour cream
	butter	2 tbsp.	wheat germ
¼ cup	white wine	1 cup	sharp Cheddar cheese
3 cups	flat noodles		

Chop broccoli, mushrooms and onion and sauté in butter until tender. Stir in wine. Boil noodles in slightly salted water until just tender. Beat eggs in a large bowl and whisk in cottage or ricotta cheese and sour cream. Add sautéed vegetables, noodles and two tablespoons of wheat germ. Mix thoroughly. Spread mixture into a buttered 9" x 13" baking pan. Sprinkle with grated Cheddar cheese and additional wheat germ and cover pan. Bake at 350°F for 30 minutes; remove the cover and bake an additional 15 minutes. Serve with tossed salad and a crispy bread.

Daniel Compton, M.L.A.
Fourth Queens
Prince Edward Island

Lobster Omelette Loaf

5 oz.	can lobster (cooked whitefish can be added, if more fish is desired. The whitefish will take on the lobster taste)	1 cup	milk
		1 cup	bread crumbs
		2	eggs, well beaten (use 3 eggs if the extra fish is used)
10 oz.	can mushroom soup		salt, pepper to taste

Mix all ingredients together. Bake in a greased loaf tin in 350°F oven until omelette is set, 25-30 minutes.

Hon. Orville H. Phillips, DDS
Senate
Prince Edward Island

Delicious Stuffed Salad Buns

1 lb.	minced lean pork	2 tsp.	flour
1 lb.	minced lean veal	¼ cup	dry mustard
¼ tsp.	soft butter	2 tbsp.	Worcestershire sauce
2	large onions, finely chopped	¼ cup	chili sauce
	salt, pepper and garlic to taste	¼ cup	finely chopped celery
		½ cup	finely chopped green pepper
10 oz.	can Campbell's Chicken Gumbo Soup	¼ tbsp.	ground parsley
		24	salad buns or hot dog buns

Sauté meat and brown in butter. Add onion, salt, pepper and garlic. Cover and cook for 30 minutes, stirring often. Add soup with flour mixed in, mustard, Worcestershire sauce, chili sauce, celery, green pepper and parsley. Cook 15 minutes, stirring occasionally. Then put mixture in salad buns. Wrap buns in foil and bake for 10 minutes in 350°F oven. May be eaten immediately or frozen for future use.

*Delicious as a light lunch or late night snack.

Barry and Cheryl Moore
Barry Moore, M.P.
Pontiac-Gatineau-Labelle
Québec

Flower Egg Stew

2	onions, thinly sliced	pinch	dill weed
2 tbsp.	butter	1	clove garlic
¾ cup	apple juice	2	whole cloves, heads removed
2½ cups	tomatoes, finely chopped	½ tsp.	basil
1	bay leaf	8	eggs, hard-boiled

Sauté onions in butter. Add apple juice and simmer until juice is reduced by half. Add remaining ingredients except eggs; simmer gently ½ hour. Cut eggs in quarters and add to sauce. Heat thoroughly. Serve over hot, buttered, whole-grain toast. Serves 6.

Marcel Tremblay, M.P.
Québec-East
Québec

Mexican Egg Bake

1 lb.	fresh mushrooms, sliced		salt and pepper
1	large onion, diced	2 cups	grated medium Cheddar
½	large green pepper, diced		cheese
	butter	2 cups	grated mozzarella or brick
1 lb.	pkg. pork sausages		cheese
10	eggs	½ cup	mild Mexican Jalapeño sauce
½ cup	sour cream		

Butter a 9" x 13" shallow baking dish. Sauté mushrooms, onions and pepper in a small amount of butter. Remove from pan. Sauté sausages in the same pan, breaking into small pieces as they cook. Drain on paper towels. Combine eggs and sour cream with a whisk. Cook eggs in a small amount of butter until shirred. Eggs must not be completely cooked. Spoon mushroom mixture and sausage pieces into the baking dish. Cover with egg mixture. Season lightly with salt and pepper. Cool. Cover with grated cheese. Bake immediately at this point or wrap in plastic wrap and refrigerate for up to 24 hours. Bake in 325°F oven for 30 minutes or until bubbling. Remove from oven. Gently spread on Jalapeño sauce. Extra sauce may be offered. Serves 8-10. Do not freeze.

Hon. David Russell, M.L.A.
Calgary - Elbow
Alberta

Breakfast-In-One

	slices of bread, crusts off	6	eggs
	cooked ham or bacon	3 cups	milk
	sharp cheese		Tabasco and Worcestershire,
	mushrooms and/or green		optional
	pepper		cornflakes

Prepare night before. In greased 9" x 13" baking dish layer: bread slices, meat, cheese, vegetable, slices of bread. Beat well eggs, milk and seasonings. Pour over layers and soak 8 hours or overnight. In the morning, sprinkle cornflakes on top and bake at 350°F for 1 hour. This freezes well. Serves 6-8.

Jack and Bunny Scowen
Jack Scowen, M.P.
Mackenzie
Saskatchewan

Quick and Easy Crêpes À La Brayonne

1 cup	milk		1 tsp.	Magic baking powder
1	egg		1 pinch	salt
1 cup	flour			

With wire whip, whip milk and egg, then add dry ingredients. Whip until smooth.
Cook in a hot cast-iron pan with a little butter or margarine until golden brown. Serve with maple sugar, syrup or melted brown sugar. Makes 4-10 crêpes.
NOTE: 2 tablespoons less flour plus ¼ cup wheat germ may be substituted, for a more substantial crêpe.

Hon. Fernand G. Dubé, Q.C., M.L.A.
Campbellton
New Brunswick

Patrick's Perfect Pancakes

1½ cups	buckwheat flour		1¾ cups	milk
3 tsp.	baking powder		2 tbsp.	melted shortening
½ tsp.	salt		2 tbsp.	honey (buckwheat honey, if
1	egg			available)

Mix together flour, baking powder and salt. Beat together egg, milk, shortening and honey. Stir in dry ingredients, beating until smooth; let stand for 2 minutes. Pour batter on to preheated greased griddle, using about ¼ cup batter for each pancake. Turn when bubbles break on the surface.
Serve hot with unsalted butter, Canadian maple syrup and a big smile. Makes about 12 pancakes.

J. Patrick Boyer, M.P.
Etobicoke-Lakeshore
Ontario

Buttermilk Pancakes

2 cups	buttermilk		2 tbsp.	oil
2 tbsp.	sugar		2 cups	flour
2	eggs		1 tsp.	soda

Mix all together. It may be lumpy but do not overmix. Cook on hot griddle. These are delicious served with any toppings.

Hon. Gordon Lank, M.L.A.
Second Queens
Prince Edward Island

Scottish Pancakes

2 cups	flour		pinch	salt
1 cup	sugar		2	eggs
1 tsp.	soda		½ cup	melted margarine
1-1½ tsp.	cream of tartar		¾ cup	milk, approximately

Combine dry ingredients, then mix in eggs and margarine. Mix in enough milk to be able to drop by tablespoon into lightly oiled electric frying pan.

Hon. Robert Muir
The Senate
Nova Scotia

Waffles

4	large eggs		5 tsp.	baking powder
2¼ cups	milk		1 tsp.	salt
1½ tsp.	vanilla		2 tbsp.	sugar
3 cups	flour		⅔ cup	melted butter

Beat eggs, milk and vanilla together in electric mixer. Combine flour, baking powder, salt and sugar, add to egg mixture. Beat until smooth, add butter. Bake in waffle iron.

Blaine Thacker, M.P.
Lethbridge-Foothills
Alberta

Bannock

| 3 cups | flour | dash | salt |
| 4 tsp. | baking powder | | water |

Preheat enough fat in frying pan on medium heat to cover bottom ¼" deep. Combine the 3 ingredients. Add enough water to make a thick sticky dough. Spoon into fat to make a pancake-shaped bannock. Turn over after golden brown. Add fat between each frying.

Thomas and Neevee Suluk
Thomas Suluk, M.P.
Nunatsiag
Northwest Territories

Hot Herb Bread

	French bread, unsliced	½ tsp.	salt
1 cup	butter	½ tsp.	paprika
½ tsp.	savory	dash	of cayenne
¾ tsp.	thyme		a little parsley for colour

Cut 1" slices nearly through to the crust. Combine butter, herbs and spices. Butter both sides of each slice. Wrap loaf in foil, put in 375°F oven for 20 minutes.

Chuck & Dale Cook
Chuck Cook, M.P.
North Vancouver-Burnaby
British Columbia

Ever-Ready Refrigerator Bran Muffins

These muffins have a beautiful shape and a light flavour.

5 cups	all-purpose flour	4 cups	buttermilk or sour milk
5 tsp.	baking soda	3	eggs
3 cups	natural bran	2 cups	Alberta honey
3 cups	All-Bran cereal	1 cup	vegetable oil
2 cups	raisins	1¼ cups	water

Sift together flour and baking soda. Add bran, cereal and raisins. Mix buttermilk, eggs, honey, oil and water together and add to dry ingredients. Stir only until moistened.

Allow batter to rest in refrigerator for 1 day.

Bake as needed at 400°F for 20 minutes. This can be stored in an ice cream pail and keeps in refrigerator for a month. Makes about 6 dozen muffins.

Frank Appleby, M.L.A.
Athabasca
Alberta

Bran Muffins

Mrs. Bennett frequently makes this recipe up in the form of a loaf from which the Minister slices off the portion he wants — for an occasional snack at the office.

1 cup	molasses	1 tsp.	salt
2	eggs	1 tsp.	baking powder
¾ cup	vegetable oil	2 tsp.	baking soda
2 cups	whole-wheat flour (soft)	2 cups	2% milk
1½ cups	natural bran	1 cup	raisins
½ cup	wheat germ		

Beat well with whisk the molasses, eggs, and oil. Blend in well the next 7 ingredients with whisk, then with spoon fold in raisins. Cover and refrigerate overnight. Batter will keep in refrigerator 1 week. Bake 20 minutes at 400°F in centre of oven using large paper cups. Makes 2 dozen large muffins, or 1 loaf.

Hon. Claude Bennett, M.P.P.
Ottawa South
Ontario

Favourite Bran Muffins

½ cup	dates or raisins	1 cup	sour milk
1 cup	flour	1 cup	crushed bran flakes
1	egg	1 tsp.	soda
1 cup	sugar	1 tsp.	cinnamon
½ cup	shortening or margarine	½ tsp.	salt

Coat the fruit with a little flour. Beat egg and add sugar and shortening. Combine sour milk, bran flakes and soda. Mix cinnamon, salt and flour, and then combine these ingredients, and the sour milk mixture to the egg and sugar mixture. Lastly, add raisins or dates and mix. Bake at 350°F in muffin tins. Instead of greasing the pan, paper cupcake liners work well.

NOTE: I have my own mill and so use stone ground flour, which for this recipe requires about 1⅓ cup of flour instead of 1 cup of regular flour.

Hon. Connie Osterman, M.L.A.
Three Hills
Alberta

Meal-In-A-Muffin

Great during a hectic political campaign.

1¼ cups	all-purpose flour	½ cup	honey
3 tsp.	baking powder	½ cup	currants
1½ cups	natural bran	½ cup	sunflower seeds
4 tbsp.	wheat germ		rind of 1 orange
1½ cups	milk	1	small carrot, grated (or nuts,
1	egg		dates, raisins, or anything
⅓ cup	vegetable oil		else handy)

Preheat oven to 400°F. Mix first 4 ingredients. Combine next 4 ingredients and add to dry mixture. Let sit 3 minutes. Add rest of ingredients and mix just enough to blend. Bake 15-20 minutes. Makes 12 good-sized muffins.

Reg and Margaret Stackhouse
Reg Stackhouse, M.P.
Scarborough West
Ontario

Carrot Zucchini Muffins

1-1¼ cups	all-purpose flour		2	large eggs
½ tbsp.	baking powder		⅓ cup	vegetable oil
¼ tsp.	baking soda		¾ cup	lightly packed, brown sugar
½ tsp.	salt		¼ cup	buttermilk
½ tbsp.	cinnamon		1 tsp.	vanilla
⅛ tsp.	nutmeg		½ cup	finely shredded zucchini
½ cup	golden raisins		½ cup	finely shredded carrot

Preheat oven to 350°F and prepare 12 muffin cups. Combine dry ingredients and raisins in a large bowl. In a medium bowl beat eggs lightly and stir in all remaining ingredients. Add moist mixture to dry mixture all at once and stir just until dry ingredients are moistened. Fill muffin cups completely full. Bake for 30 minutes. Makes 12 muffins.

Gerry and Margaret St. Germain
Gerry St. Germain, M.P.
Mission-Port Moody
British Columbia

Apple Muffins

¼ cup	soft shortening		¾ tsp.	baking soda
¾ cup	well-packed brown sugar		1 tsp.	baking powder
1	egg, slightly beaten		¾ tsp.	salt
1-1½ cups	grated or chopped apple		¼ tsp.	cinnamon
1 tbsp.	10% cream		¼ tsp.	nutmeg
½ cup	raisins (optional)			sugar
1 cup	all-purpose or whole-wheat flour			cinnamon

Cream together shortening and brown sugar. Add egg, apple, cream and raisins, if used, and beat mixture. Sift together next 6 ingredients into apple mixture. Stir until moistened and drop into buttered muffin tins. Sprinkle sugar and cinnamon on top. Bake at 375°F for 20 minutes.

Hon. Pat Carney, P.C., M.P.
Vancouver Centre
British Columbia

Best Bran Muffins

This recipe is a great family favourite with both donors.

3 cups	white sugar	5 cups	flour
1 cup	margarine	4 cups	bran flakes cereal
4	eggs	3 tbsp.	baking soda
4 cups	buttermilk	1 tsp.	salt
2 cups	Health Bran soaked in 2 cups boiling water	2 cups	raisins or dates

Cream sugar, margarine and eggs. Add buttermilk and Health Bran which has been soaked in boiling water. Allow to cool. Combine next 4 ingredients and add, then stir in raisins. Store in refrigerator in covered container. Do not use the first day. This batter keeps for 1 month.

To make muffins, fill prepared muffin pans and bake in preheated 350°F oven until done, about 20-25 minutes.

Hon. Dr. Neil Webber, M.L.A.
Calgary Bow
Alberta
and
Myrna C. Fyfe, M.L.A.
St. Albert
Alberta

Ma's Spread

To enjoy the following recipe, you will need children, a summer picnic setting, and fresh home-baked bread.

Take equal parts of peanut butter, Cheddar cheese and H.P. Sauce to taste. Mix the spread well. Pack the sandwiches carefully to keep them moist.

Take along a jug of lemonade. You will have a great day!

Hon. Richard J. Doyle,
The Senate
Québec

Zwieback

Here is a recipe which is of Russian Mennonite origin.

2 cups	scalded milk		1	pkg. yeast
½ cup	butter		2 tsp.	sugar
½ cup	shortening		1 cup	warm water
2 tsp.	salt		8-10 cups	all-purpose flour
4 tbsp.	sugar			

Scald milk, add butter and shortening, salt and the 4 tablespoons sugar. Put yeast in a small bowl, add 2 tsp. sugar and 1 cup warm water. Set in a warm place until spongy. Add yeast mixture to warm milk. Mix well and stir in flour gradually. Knead dough until very soft and smooth. Cover and let rise in warm place until double in bulk. Pinch off small balls of dough the size of a small egg. Place 1" apart on greased pan. Put a smaller bun on top of each bun and press down with thumb. Let rise again until double in bulk about 1 hour. Bake at 400°F for 15-20 minutes. Yields 4 dozen.

John, Mary, Ann and Mike Reimer
John Reimer, M.P.
Kitchener
Ontario

Zucchini Bread

2	eggs		2 cups	flour
½ cup	cooking oil		1 tsp.	baking powder
1 cup	granulated sugar		1 tsp.	baking soda
1 cup	grated unpeeled zucchini		½ tsp.	salt
1 tsp.	vanilla		1 tsp.	cinnamon

Beat eggs until frothy, beat in oil and sugar, stir in zucchini and vanilla.

In a separate bowl put remaining 5 dry ingredients and stir well. Pour into zucchni mixture, stir to moisten. Pour into greased 9" x 5" x 3" loaf pan.

Bake in 350°F oven for 50 to 60 minutes. Let stand 10 minutes, remove from pan and cool on rack. Yields 1 loaf.

Hon. J. Robert Howie, P.C., Q.C., M.P.
York-Sunbury
New Brunswick

Biscuit Supreme

2 cups	flour		2 tsp.	sugar
4 tsp.	baking powder		½ cup	shortening
½ tsp.	salt		¾ cup	milk
½ tsp.	cream of tartar			

Sift dry ingredients into bowl. Cut in shortening until like coarse crumbs. Make a well. Add milk all at once. Stir quickly with a fork just until dough follows fork around bowl.

Turn onto lightly floured surface. (Dough should be soft). Knead gently 10 to 12 strokes. Roll or pat dough ½" thick. Dip biscuit cutter in flour. Cut out biscuits. Bake on ungreased baking sheet in 450°F oven for 10-12 minutes. Makes about 16 medium-sized biscuits.

Hon. Prowse G. Chappell, M.L.A.
Fourth Prince
Prince Edward Island

Welsh Cakes

3 cups	unsifted all-purpose flour		¼ tsp.	ground mace
1½ tsp.	baking powder		1 cup	shortening or butter
½ tsp.	baking soda		¾ cup	currants
1 tsp.	salt		¼ cup	finely chopped mixed peel
1 cup	sugar		2	eggs, beaten
1 tsp.	ground nutmeg		6 tbsp.	milk

Sift dry ingredients in bowl. Cut in fat finely. Add fruit. Add eggs mixed with milk to make stiff dough. Roll to ¼" thickness on floured surface (roll out ½ the dough at a time). Cut rounds with 2" cookie cutter. Bake on heated griddle on low heat or in electric frying pan at 250°F for 8-10 minutes. Turn and brown other side.

Gary and Liz Lane
Hon. J. Gary Lane, M.L.A.
Qu'Appelle-Lumsden
Saskatchewan

Hard Oat Bread

This bread has been passed down in Fred's family for over 3 generations.

1 cup	butter	½ cup	boiling water
4 cups	oatmeal	1 tsp.	salt

Put butter in centre of bowl and surround it with the oatmeal. Add boiling water and salt and mix all together. Turn out on board sprinkled with oatmeal and roll with rolling pin to a thickness of ½" or less. (The thinner it is rolled, the "crispier" it will be). Cut in squares and bake in hot oven (375°-400°F) until golden brown. We find this is great with baked beans.

Fred and Marjorie McCain
Fred McCain, M.P.
Carleton-Charlotte
New Brunswick

Scottish Raisin Bran Loaf

1 cup	flour	1 cup	bran
1 tsp.	baking powder	1 cup	raisins
1 cup	brown sugar	1 cup	milk

Mix all ingredients together, pour into greased loaf pan. Bake at 350°F for 1 hour or until straw comes out clean. This recipe is fast, easy and freezes well.
NOTE: If doubling recipe, use only 1½ cups brown sugar.

Hon. Flora MacDonald, P.C., M.P.
Kingston and the Islands
Ontario

White Bread and Rolls

My home is in Ancaster, Ontario and one of the oldest and possibly best-preserved operating grist mills in Canada is the Ancaster Old Mill. It was originally built in 1792 and has been replaced and rebuilt in 1863 after a fire.

Given this history, I thought that my contribution to your cookbook should reflect something of my area.

1 tsp.	sugar	¼ cup	sugar
½ cup	lukewarm water	1 tbsp.	salt
1 pkg.	active dry yeast	¼ cup	shortening
1 cup	hot milk	5½-6 cups	all-purpose flour
½ cup	warm water		

Dissolve 1 tsp. sugar in ½ cup water and sprinkle yeast over top. Let stand 10 minutes. Combine milk, ½ cup water, ¼ cup sugar, salt and shortening. Stir until shortening melts and cool to lukewarm. Stir in yeast mixture. Gradually beat in 3 cups flour. Work in enough remaining flour to make soft dough. Turn onto floured board and kneed until smooth and elastic, 8 to 10 minutes. Shape in ball and place in greased bowl, turning to grease top. Cover and let rise in warm place, free from drafts, until double in bulk, about 1½ hours. Punch down, divide in half, cover and let rest 10 minutes. Shape in 2 loaves and place in greased 2-quart loaf pans (9" x 5" x 3"), or shape in rolls and place in greased baking pans for pan rolls; or greased large muffin tins for individual rolls. Brush with melted fat. Cover and let stand in warm place until double in bulk, about 1½ hours.

Bake loaves 30 to 35 minutes, pan rolls 20 to 25 minutes and individual rolls 15 to 20 minutes at 375°F. Makes 2 loaves or 24 rolls.

Ann Sloat, M.P.P.
Wentworth North
Ontario.

Whole-Wheat Bread

1 pkg.	yeast		4 cups	water
½ cup	lukewarm water		½ cup	margarine
1 tsp.	sugar		¼ cup	honey
6 cups	whole-wheat flour		4-5 cups	white flour
4 tsp.	salt			

Dissolve package of yeast in ½ cup lukewarm water and 1 tsp. sugar. Let stand while preparing other ingredients. Put whole-wheat flour and salt into large bowl and mix. Make a well in centre, and add water, margarine, honey and yeast.

Stir with wooden spoon until well mixed. Add white flour slowly and work into a firm but soft dough. Cover and let rise until double in bulk. Punch down and let rise again. Put dough on floured surface and divide into equal parts. Cover; let rest 10 minutes. Form into loaves; place in well-greased pans. Let rise until almost double in size. Bake in 375°F oven 1 hour. Makes 4 loaves.

Wally and Hilda McKenzie
Wally McKenzie, M.L.A.
Roblin-Russell
Manitoba

Cornmeal Bread

This bread goes well with baked ham and a tossed salad. It can also be served hot as a side dish with golden syrup and butter.

1 cup	flour		1 cup	milk
1 cup	cornmeal		½ cup	water
3 tbsp.	sugar		2	eggs
2 tsp.	baking powder		½ cup	oil or shortening
1 tsp.	salt			

Mix dry ingredients in a bowl. Mix liquids and add all at once to dry ingredients. Mix with as few strokes as possible. Pour into greased and floured 8" x 8" pan. Bake in preheated oven at 375°F for 25-30 minutes.

Stan and Eileen Graham
Stan Graham, M.P.
Kootenay East-Revelstoke Riding
British Columbia

Brown Bread

1 tsp.	sugar		1 tbsp.	molasses
1 cup	lukewarm water		4 cups	Robin Hood white flour
2 pkg.	yeast		1 cup	whole-wheat flour
4 tbsp.	sugar		1 cup	rye flour
1 tbsp.	salt			handful cracked-wheat or 5-
5 tbsp.	melted bacon fat			grain cereal
	OR vegetable oil		3-4 cups	Robin Hood white flour
4 cups	lukewarm liquid			

Dissolve 1 tsp. sugar in 1 cup lukewarm water. Add yeast, let stand 10 minutes. Meantime, in a large bowl combine 4 tbsp. sugar, salt and bacon fat or oil. Stir in 4 cups of lukewarm liquid: 3½ cups warm water OR potato water and ½ cup milk. Add molasses and 4 cups white flour. Stir yeast and add. Stir in whole wheat and rye flours. Add cereal. Stir in 3 or 4 cups white flour or enough to handle dough, knead 10 minutes. Set in greased bowl, let rise in oven for 1 hour. Punch down. Let rise again, shape into 4 loaves. Let rise until above pans, approximately 1 hour in oven away from drafts. Bake 15 minutes at 400°F, then 25 minutes at 325°F. Cool loaves on side on racks.

L. Greenaway, M.P.
Cariboo-Chilcotin
British Columbia

Rye Bread

2 tbsp.	yeast		4 tbsp.	oil
1 tsp.	sugar		4 tbsp.	corn syrup
½ cup	warm water		1 tbsp.	salt
4 cups	lukewarm water		8-9 cups	white flour
1 cup	brown sugar		3 cups	rye flour

Dissolve yeast in sweetened warm water. Let stand 10 minutes and then add to a mixture of the next 5 ingredients. Stir in about 6 cups of the white flour. Let stand as a sponge for ½ hour. Add rye flour plus enough white flour, 2-3 cups, to make a stiff dough. Let rise 2 hours. Punch down. Let rise 1 hour. Form into flat loaves. Let rise 1 hour again. Bake 20 minutes at 350°F.

Michael Hopfner, M.L.A.
Cut Knife-Lloydminster
Saskatchewan

Kolach (Ukrainian Christmas Bread)

1 tsp.	sugar		1 tbsp.	salt
½ cup	warm water		½ cup	sugar
2 pkg.	yeast		4 tbsp.	oil
½ cup	lukewarm water		8½ cups	all-purpose flour
4	eggs, beaten			

Dissolve sugar in warm water, sprinkle on yeast and let rise 10 minutes. Combine yeast with next 5 ingredients, then mix in the flour. Knead until smooth and dough leaves hand (a little stiffer than bread dough). Cover and let rise in a warm spot until doubled. Punch down and let rise again.

Divide dough into 4 portions.

Grease 2, 9" x 2" round pans. Take 1 part of dough and divide into 5 equal parts. Roll out 3 parts to 36 inches long (twice the thickness of a pencil). Braid these lengths. Join ends and place in pan leaving a 1" space around edge of pan.

Starting at the centre, entwine the other 2 lengths, working left to right. Turn and repeat. Join ends and place in the 1" space next to the braid.

Divide the second portion into 6 equal pieces. Roll each piece to 38" (same thickness as above). Starting at centre, entwine 2 pieces working from left to right. Turn and repeat. Do the same to remaining pieces. (You now have 3 pieces.)

Starting at centre, take the 2 entwined lengths that are on the left and the lengths that are on the right. Repeat until half is entwined. Turn and repeat.

Brush base with water.

Join the entwined length and place on base, making an even circle. Press lightly. Put in a warm spot to rise until almost double.

Glaze with 1 beaten egg. Bake at 350°F for 45 minutes.

Hon. Steve Paproski, P.C., M.P.
Edmonton North
Alberta

Raisin Bread

1½ cups	milk		¼ cup	flour
1½ cups	water		2 tsp.	nutmeg
1 tsp.	shortening		7-8 cups	white flour
1 tsp.	salt		1 tbsp.	yeast
¼ cup	molasses		1 tsp.	sugar
1	egg, beaten		1 cup	lukewarm water
1 lb.	seedless raisins			

Scald first 5 ingredients, then cool to lukewarm. Add egg, raisins mixed with the ¼ cup flour and nutmeg. Sprinkle yeast over sugared water. Let rise, about 5 minutes. Mix flour into scalded mixture, then mix in dissolved yeast. Let rise until double in bulk, then set in pans. Let rise again until double in bulk. Bake at 325°F for 35-40 minutes.

Hon. Wilbur MacDonald, M.L.A.
Fifth Queens
Prince Edward Island

Coffee Cake

½ cup	butter or margarine		1 tsp.	soda
1 cup	white sugar		1 tsp.	baking powder
2	eggs		1 cup	sour cream
2 cups	cake flour		1 tsp.	vanilla

Topping and Filling:

¾ cup	brown sugar		1 cup	finely chopped nuts
1 tsp.	cinnamon			

Cream butter, add sugar slowly. Add eggs, beating well after each egg. Sift flour, soda and baking powder together. Add alternately to creamed mixture along with sour cream. Fold in vanilla last. Grease and flour 9" x 12" cake pan. Pour half of batter into pan.

Combine topping and filling ingredients. Pour half of filling over half of batter. Repeat with batter and topping. Bake at 375°F for 30-40 minutes.

Robert and Marian Fischer
Robert Fischer, M.L.A.
Wainwright
Alberta

Little Coffee Cakes (Kleina Kaffee Kushen)

1	yeast cake	3 tbsp.	sugar
¼ cup	cup cream or milk	1 tsp.	salt
3 cups	flour, sifted	2	whole eggs
½ cup	shortening (half butter)	2	2 egg yolks

Dissolve yeast cake in ¼ cup warm cream or milk, add 2 tbsp. flour and let stand in warm place to rise. Cream butter and sugar, add salt and the eggs, beaten in 1 at a time. Add the sponge containing the yeast, then add the sifted flour. Grease muffin pans and sift a little flour over them. Fill pans about ⅔ full with the batter. Set in a warm place until dough rises to the top of the pans. Bake in a hot oven, about 400°F, for 25 minutes.

Andrew Witer, M.P.
Parkdale-High Park
Ontario

Soups and Salads

Squash Soup

1	med. squash, peeled, seeded, chopped		butter
		2 tbsp.	sherry
4 cups	chicken stock		flour
1 tbsp.	tarragon	1 cup	med. cream
1 tbsp.	plus parsley		salt and pepper
1	large onion, diced		celery salt
1	garlic clove, crushed		sour cream or yogurt

Put squash in pan. Add just enough broth to cover squash. Add tarragon and parsley, cover and cook until soft. Sauté onions and garlic in butter and sherry until soft. Add flour to onions and simmer for 1 minute, allowing 1½ tbsp. flour for each cup of stock used in cooking squash. Add onion mixture to squash pan and simmer until thickened. Purée until velvety smooth in blender. Add cream and season just before serving. Garnish with dollop of sour cream or plain yogurt and fresh parsley. Makes 8-9 cups.

Stewart McInnes, M.P.
Halifax
Nova Scotia

Carrot Soup

2	onions, peeled and chopped	2	bunches fresh carrots
2 tbsp.	butter	1	potato, peeled and grated
5 cups	chicken stock (or enough to cover carrots)	dash	cayenne pepper
		½ cup	cream (optional)

Sauté onions in butter until tender. Add stock and carrots. Boil until tender. Add grated potato during last 5 minutes. Remove from stove and purée all ingredients in food processor. Add cayenne to taste. Reheat and add ½ cup cream, if desired. Garnish with chives or parsley.

Peter and Geraldine Peterson
Peter Peterson, M.P.
Hamilton West
Ontario

Russian Borscht

2 lbs.	soup meat and bones		parsley, chopped
	water		salt
1	large onion, chopped	10 oz.	can tomato soup OR 14 oz.
1	small head cabbage, chopped		can tomatoes, crushed
4	medium potatoes, cubed	1 cup	sweet cream, optional
	dill, chopped		sour cream, optional

Cover soup meat and bones with water. Simmer 2-3 hours. Skim. Add onion, cabbage, potatoes. Simmer until vegetables are tender. Add dill, parsley and salt to taste. Add tomato soup or tomatoes. Simmer for 10 minutes. If you wish, add sweet cream just before serving or top each bowl with sour cream. This soup improves with reheating.

Benno and Marge Friesen
Benno Friesen, M.P.
Surrey-White Rock-North Delta
British Columbia

Bill's Borscht

1 cup	carrots	3 tbsp.	cooking oil
2 cups	beets	1 cup	cabbage, shredded
1 cup	celery, diced	½ cup	fresh or dried mushrooms
2	med. onions, finely chopped	2 cups	tomato juice
	salt to taste	1 tbsp.	lemon juice
10	whole peppercorns	2 tbsp.	cornstarch
2	bay leaves	½ cup	flour
6½ cups	water	1 tsp.	oil

Grate carrots and beets on medium-sized grater. Add diced celery, 1 chopped onion, salt, peppercorns and bay leaves in cheesecloth, cold water and simmer for ½ hour. Fry other chopped onion in oil until light in colour. Add cabbage and mushrooms. Simmer until all vegetables are tender but firm. Add tomato and lemon juice. Dissolve cornstarch in ¼ cup cold water and add to borscht.

Meanwhile, mix flour, oil and enough water to make soft dough and roll to the thickness of a pencil. Cut in ¼" pieces, add to borscht and boil for 2 minutes. Serve.

Hon. Bill Diachuk, M.L.A.
Edmonton Beverly
Alberta

Borscht with Spring Beets

8	small beets with tops	1	clove garlic
6 cups	soup stock	½ cup	tomato juice
5 cups	water	1 tbsp.	ketchup
1	medium potato, diced		lemon juice
1	medium onion, chopped		honey
1	medium carrot, diced	1 tbsp.	chopped dill
½ cup	diced string beans		table cream
1	small celery, diced		salt and pepper
2 cups	shredded cabbage		

Wash beets thoroughly. Cut beets (do not pare) into thin strips and cut tops into small pieces. Pour the soup stock and water together with the beets and vegetables into pot. Cook until vegetables are tender. Pour in tomato juice and ketchup. Add several drops of lemon juice and some honey for a sweet-sour taste. Bring to a boil. Add dill and cream to taste, then season with salt and pepper according to taste.

Hon. Paul Yuzyk
The Senate
Manitoba

Broccoli and Cheddar Soup

2	bunches broccoli, coarsely chopped	2	bay leaves
		1½ cups	ale
4 cups	chicken stock or broth	1 cup	grated sharp Cheddar
2 cups	heavy cream		salt, pepper, Tabasco to taste

In a large sucepan, simmer the broccoli in the stock, covered partially, for 20 minutes or until tender. Purée the broccoli mixture in the food processor in batches and return mixture to pan. In a saucepan, scald the cream with the bay leaves; add the ale in a slow stream, stirring and bring the mixture to a simmer. Add the Cheddar, a little at a time, stirring until the Cheddar is melted and remove the pan from the heat. Add Cheddar mixture to the broccoli purée, heat over moderate heat — do not let boil. Add salt, pepper and Tabasco to taste. Ladle into heated bowls.

Tom and Mary Hockin
Tom Hockin, M.P.
London West
Ontario

Kate's Clam Chowder

3	slices bacon	½ tsp.	dill or fennel
2	sticks celery	½ tsp.	curry powder
1	medium onion	1	chicken stock cube
5 oz.	can clams	3	potatoes, diced
1	bay leaf	1 cup	water
dash	pepper	dash	garlic powder
			juice of ½ lemon

Chop bacon, celery and onion in ½" bits. Fry bacon until transparent, then add onion, celery and sauté until softened. Add the juice from the clams and the remaining ingredients. Simmer, covered, for ½ hour. Add the clams for a few minutes at the end.

I serve in warmed soup bowls with a dab of butter, sprinkling of parsley and lots of hot garlic bread. Add fresh oysters and whitefish for a really hearty feed.

Ted, Kate, Meghan and Simon Schellenberg
Ted Schellenberg, M.P.
Nanaimo - Alberni
British Columbia

Down East Clam Chowder

4	slices side bacon	2½ cups	milk
½ cup	finely chopped onion	1 tsp.	salt
2 cups	diced potatoes	½ tsp.	celery salt
1 cup	boiling water	⅛ tsp.	pepper
2 x 5 oz.	cans clams		paprika to taste

Fry finely diced bacon in a large saucepan. Remove bacon and set aside. Pour off all but 2 tbsp. of fat. Fry onions until transparent. Add potatoes and boiling water, boil about 10 minutes. Add clams and all remaining ingredients. Stir well to combine and heat on low until well heated.

If a thicker chowder is desired, mix 3 tbsp. flour and ¼ cup milk to a paste and combine with about 1 cup of the chowder broth, then stir back into the chowder.

Always keep at low heat so as not to curdle. Yields 8½ cups.

J. Michael Forrestall, M.P.
Dartmouth - Halifax East
Nova Scotia

C.W.'s Fundy Chowder

1 tbsp.	butter	5 oz.	can whole oysters (not smoked)
5 oz.	can baby clams		
1	can Snow's Clam Chowder	3	clam tins of milk
			pepper

Melt butter in a pot, add other ingredients. Heat slowly. Use your own discretion as to what portion of brine you add to chowder or drain off clams and oysters.
NOTE: You could add: 10 oz. can mushroom pieces, leftover potatoes, chopped onions and/or scallops.
Serves 4 or more.

Hon. C. W. E. Harmer, M.L.A.
Petitcodiac
New Brunswick

St. James Clam Chowder

2 x 5 oz.	cans baby clams	3	potatoes (2" diameter), chopped in ½" cubes
1	Spanish onion (3" diameter), finely chopped	1 tbsp.	finely chopped fresh green pepper
½ lb.	sliced back bacon, cut in ½" squares	¼ tsp.	pepper
¼ cup	butter or margarine	½ tsp.	salt
6 cups	water	1 cup	milk
		½ cup	flour

Drain off clam juice, set aside, and let settle for 5 minutes. Wash clams in colander under tap, set aside. Sauté onions and back bacon in ¼ cup of butter in large soup pot. Add clam juice draining carefully, leaving shells, etc. for waste. Add washed clams, 6 cups water, potatoes, onion, green pepper, salt and pepper. Gently boil for 40 minutes. Take off heat for 5 minutes to cool and then add milk. Take ½ cup of flour in separate container and add small amount of cold water and stir till smooth. Stir into soup and place on heat and return to boil. Stir till thickened. Serves approximately 8 people. Individuals can add salt and pepper to their own taste.

George Minaker, M.P.
Winnipeg - St. James
Manitoba

Cod Chowder

1½-2 lbs.	fresh or frozen cod	1	bay leaf
2 tbsp.	butter	10 oz.	can celery soup,
2	small onions, chopped		undiluted
4	sticks celery, finely chopped	1½ cups	fresh milk
2 tbsp.	flour		salt and pepper
1	large potato, chopped	½ cup	commercial sour cream
			chives

Poach fish for about 5 minutes or until it flakes. Drain fish, remove bones, save 1½ cups liquid. In large pot, melt butter and sauté onions and celery until soft. Do not brown. Add flour, fish stock and potato. Mix well. Add bay leaf, cover and cook slowly about 10 minutes or until potato is soft. Stir occasionally to keep from sticking.

Remove bay leaf. Add celery soup and milk. Add salt and pepper to taste. Add flaked fish and cover. Simmer for about 15 minutes. Remove from heat. Can be left standing for hours if necessary. Just before serving, add sour cream and heat just to boiling. Sprinkle with chives and serve. Serves 6-8.

Hon. Dr. Hugh Twomey, M. D., M.H.A.
Exploits
Newfoundland and Labrador

Fresh Fish Chowder

1 lb.	fish fillets	½ cup	carrots
2 tbsp.	butter OR other fat	2 cups	boiling water
1	medium onion, thinly sliced	1 tsp.	salt
½ cup	diced celery	⅛ tsp.	pepper
2 cups	diced raw potatoes	2 cups	milk

Cut fillets into bite-sized pieces. Melt fat in large saucepan and cook onion and celery until tender. Add potatoes, carrots, water, salt and pepper. Cover and simmer 10 to 15 minutes until vegetables are tender. Add fish and cook 10 minutes longer. Add milk. Reheat but do not boil. Serves 6.

Lawrence O'Neil, M.P.
Cape Breton
Highland - Canso
Nova Scotia

Seafood Chowder

1 lb.	scallops	¾ cup	flour
1 lb.	shrimp, cleaned	1½ cups	diced potato
1 lb.	cod fillets	5 cups	milk, hot
1 lb.	onions	2½ cups	light cream, hot
1 cup	butter		salt and pepper to taste

Cut scallops ½" dice. Cover with 2½ cups water, poach 10 minutes. Remove from heat and reserve. Cut each shrimp in 4 equal pieces. Cover cod with 1 quart water, poach 7 to 8 minutes, until cooked but firm. Reserve. Sauté onions in butter, add shrimp. Cook 5 minutes or until shrimp are done. Add flour, mixing well. Cook 3 to 4 minutes but do not brown. Cook potatoes separately in 2½ cups water. Add strained cod stock to roux (onion-flour mixture) gradually, stir until thick and smooth. Add potatoes and scallops with cooking water. Bone cod, flake in pieces large enough to identify, add to chowder. Add hot milk and cream. Season to taste. Serves 25.

Hon. Len Simms, M.H.A.
Grand Falls
Newfoundland and Labrador

Premier's Chowder

1 lb.	frozen fish fillets and/or frozen shellfish*	2 cups	boiling water
1	onion, chopped	1 tsp.	salt
½ cup	chopped celery	1 tsp.	thyme
2 tbsp.	butter	dash	pepper
2 cups	diced raw potatoes	1½ cups	whole milk
½ cup	sliced carrots	¾ cup	cereal cream
			paprika

Partially thaw fillets, cut into 1" cubes. In a saucepan, sauté onion and celery in butter until tender. Add potatoes, carrots, water, salt, thyme and pepper. Cover and simmer 10 to 15 minutes until vegetables are tender. Add fish and/or scallops, if used, and cook 10 minutes longer or until flesh becomes opaque. Add milk, cream and remaining shellfish, if used, heat gently but do not boil. Sprinkle each serving with paprika. Makes 6 servings.
*cod, haddock, ocean perch, boston bluefish/shrimp, crabmeat, scallops, clams.

Hon. Jean Gauvin, M.L.A.
Shippagan-les-Iles
New Brunswick

Chowder Des Grenadines

Cette spécialité du Ministre André Bissonnette a été préparée sur un voilier lors d'un voyage aux Grenadines. Monsieur Bissonnette est un excellent cuisinier qui prendra plaisir à vous faire goûter sa cuisine si l'occasion se présente.

2	à 3 branches de céleri coupés en dés	1	tasse de pétoncles égouttés
1	petit oignon haché finement	1	petite boite de crevettes de Matane égouttées
1	feuille de laurier	3	c.à table de beurre
⅔	tasse de champignons frais ou en conserve coupés en tranches	3	c.à table de farine
		3	tasses de lait
	sel et poivre	½	tasse de crême de vin blanc
¼	tasse de beurre	2	tranches d'ananas coupées en morceaux (facultatif).
⅓	tasse de filet de poisson en cubes		

Faire mijoter dans le beurre à feu lent sans laisser brunir le céleri, l'oignon, les champignons, les pétoncles et le poisson environ 3 à 4 minutes. Saler et poivrer. Adjouter l'eau et laisser mijoter à découvert encore 4 à 5 minutes.

Retirer du feu et ajouter les crevettes et les ananas.

Faire fondre les 3 c. à table de beurre dans une casserole de 2 pintes, ajouter les 2 c. à table de farine et brasser pour mélanger farine et beurre à feu très lent sans laisser brunir. Ajouter le lait et la crême (ou le vin blanc). Chauffer le lait en brassant constamment sans laisser bouillir. Ajoûter sel et poivre et feuille de laurier.

Au moment de servir, verser le mélange légumes et poisson dans le lait chaud, servir immédiatement. Décorer chaque bol avec paprika ou persil.

NOTE: Cette recette a été préparée sur le bateau avec du poisson d'eau salée, mais on peut tout aussi bien utiliser des poissons d'eau douce à chair ferme tels: morue, doré, truite.

L'hon Andre Bissonnette, P.C., M.P.
Saint-Jean
Québec

Chicken-Egg-Lemon Soup (Soupa Avgolemono)

8 cups	chicken stock (recipe follows)	8	medium eggs, separated
½ cup	rice, uncooked	1 tsp.	water
	salt and pepper to taste		juice of 1 or 2 lemons

In a large saucepan bring chicken stock to a boil, add rice and bring again to a boil, stirring occasionally. Reduce heat to moderate, cover pan and cook until rice is soft, 15-20 minutes. Season to taste with salt and pepper. Remove from heat.

Beat egg whites, with 1 tsp. of water, until they peak. Add yolks and beat 5 minutes longer, until fluffy and light yellow. Slowly add juice of 1 lemon, beating continuously. While still beating, add ½ cup of stock, a little at a time. This is necessary to keep eggs from curdling. Pour egg mixture into soup and stir gently. Taste. Add more lemon juice if you wish. Serves 6.

Chicken Stock

4 lb.	fowl or 3½ lb. chicken parts (backs, necks, giblets)	2	celery stalks, washed and quartered
1	onion, unpeeled, quartered	5 sprigs	flat-leaf parsley
2	carrots, washed and quartered	1 tsp.	salt
		1 tsp.	pepper
		4 qt.	water

Combine all ingredients in a large pan. Bring water to a boil, skim off froth. Reduce heat to low. Cover the pot, leaving a small opening for steam to escape, and simmer 2-3 hours. Remove fat from top of stock. Discard bones and vegetables and strain rest through fine sieve. Correct seasonings.

Hon. E. W. Barootes
The Senate
Saskatchewan

French Canadian Pea Soup

2	good-sized pork hocks		salt and pepper to taste
1 lb.	pkg. yellow slit peas	3 tbsp.	flour
1 cup	finely chopped onions	3 tbsp.	butter
1 cup	finely chopped celery		

Pork hocks and peas should be placed in a soup pot with 12-14 cups water. Simmer for 3 hours.

Remove pork hocks from pot, and clean meat from bones and add it to peas. Salt and pepper to taste. Thicken with a paste of flour and butter. The soup can be eaten right away or for extra flavour let stand in refrigerator overnight.

Jack Shields, M.P.
Athabasca
Alberta

Turkey Soup

	turkey carcass, broken up	4 tbsp.	pot barley
4 tsp.	salt	¼ cup	lentils
2	chicken bouillon cubes	2 tbsp.	rice
1 cup	grated carrots	¼ cup	parsley flakes
1 cup	chopped celery	3 cups	chopped turkey
1 cup	chopped onion	1 cup	macaroni or noodles
19 oz.	can tomatoes		

Simmer carcass in 18 cups of water, with salt added, for 5 hours. Discard bones and cool broth. Lift off fat. Add remaining ingredients and simmer 2 to 3 hours.

Hon. Lorne McLaren, M.L.A.
Yorkton
Saskatchewan

Minestrone à la génoise

¼	de tasse d'huile d'olive	1	paquet de 10 oz. de haricots verts congelés
1	gousse d'ail broyée		
1	oignon haché fin	6	tasses d'eau
1	poireau lavé et coup é en dés	6	cubes de bouillon de boeuf
1	c. à table de persil	1	tasse de macaroni en doudes ou ditali
½	à thé de thym séché		
1	c. à table de páte de tomates	1	tasse de petities féves suites et égouttées
3	tomates moyennes, pelées, épépinées et hachées		Pesto, au choix
2	branches de céleri, hachées		Parmesan rápé
2	carottes coupées en dés		
2	pommes de terre coupées en dés		

Faire chauffer l'huile dans une grande casserole. Ajouter l'ail, l'oignon, le poireau, le persil et le thym; faire cuire jusqu'à transparence de l'oignon. Ajouter la páte de tomates, les tomates, le céleri, les carottes, les pommes de terre, les haricots verts, l'eau et les cubes de bouillon. Recouvrir et faire mijoter environ une heure. Amener à ébullition; ajouter le macaroni; cuire jusqu 'á ce que ce soit tendre, soit environ 8 à 10 minutes. Ajouter les petites féves. Faire chauffer. Servir avec le pesto et le Parmesan. Pour 8 personnes.

Vincent et Francine Della Noce
Vincent Della Noce, M.P.
Duvernay
Québec

Simple Soup

10 oz.	can mushroom soup	5 oz.	tin of broken shrimp
10 oz.	can cream of tomato soup	1	soup can table cream
½	soup can dry sherry		

Combine all ingredients in saucepan. Warm slowly, do not boil. Serves 8. Very rich.

Dan McKenzie, M.P.
Winnipeg - Assiniboine
Manitoba

Hamburger Soup

Don't be deceived by the name — this is a family favourite and great for entertaining. This recipe makes 18 soup ladles and it freezes very well.

1½ lbs.	ground beef	10 oz.	can tomato soup
1	medium onion, finely chopped	4	carrots, finely chopped parsley
28 oz.	can tomatoes	½ tsp.	thyme
2 cups	water		pepper to taste
3 x 10 oz.	cans consommé	½ cup	barley

Brown meat and onions, drain well. Combine all ingredients in large pot, simmer covered at least 2 hours or all day.

Hint: I use my crock pot, prepare in the morning and simmer until evening for dinner.

Bill and Lois Gottselig
Bill Gottselig, M.P.
Moose Jaw
Saskatchewan

M.L.A. Survival Tomato Soup

	Aylmer canned tomatoes	pepper
½-1 tsp.	baking soda	Tabasco, Worcestershire or
	milk	H.P. sauce, optional

Take 1 can of Aylmer canned tomatoes. Mash as smooth as possible. Add ½ to 1 tsp. of baking soda; mix and allow to simmer on stove. The soda appears to break down the acid in the tomatoes. When hot, just add an equal amount of milk. Add pepper to taste.

You may add all kinds of sauces for a special taste. Some examples are listed, but you can use your imagination and try anything you like.

Tom Lysons, M.L.A.
Vermilion-Viking
Alberta

Oxford Hunting Soup

10 oz.	can cream of mushroom soup	10 oz.	can cream of tomato soup
10 oz.	can cream of chicken soup	10 oz.	can consommé soup
10 oz.	can cream of celery soup	4	soup cans milk
			sherry to taste

Mix the soups, gradually adding milk. Cook slowly; do not boil. Add sherry to taste just before serving. Serves 8 or more.

Richard L. Treleaven, Q.C., M.P.P.
Oxford
Ontario

Lemony Pea Soup

In North Africa they use yellow split peas but green split peas are equally good.

1 cup	split peas	1 tsp.	ground cumin
1 cup	sliced celery	2-3 tbsp.	lemon juice
4 cups	chicken stock	2 tbsp.	flour
½ tsp.	salt	2 tbsp.	margarine
¼ tsp.	pepper		

Cook the peas and celery in the chicken stock for 45 minutes or until peas are tender. Purée. Add the seasonings. Add the flour to the melted margarine, use a small amount of soup to thin, add to the soup and simmer for 5 minutes. Serves 4.
Delicious with garlic bread.

John and Judy Gerich
John Gerich, M.L.A.
Redberry
Saskatchewan

Spinach Salad

1 bag	of spinach	10 oz.	can water chestnuts
¼ lb.	bacon	1	onion
2	hard-cooked eggs	1 cup	fresh bean sprouts

Dressing:

¼-½ cup	salad oil	¼ cup	cider vinegar
2 tbsp.	red wine	2 tbsp.	sugar
½ cup	ketchup	½ tsp.	salt
1 tsp.	Worcestershire sauce	1 tsp.	paprika

This salad may be made the night before. Wash spinach and break into small pieces. Fry bacon until crisp and cut into little pieces. Slice eggs, water chestnuts and onion and toss all with spinach. Combine dressing ingredients and add just before serving. Serves 4-6.

Hon. Elmer MacKay, P.C., M.P.
Central Nova
Nova Scotia

Layered Salad

	lettuce		grated cheese
	onions		cut-up celery
	radish	2 cups	mayonnaise
	peas and carrots (frozen)	1 tbsp.	prepared mustard
2 tbsp.	sugar	1	hard-boiled egg

Layer first 7 ingredients in serving bowl. Combine mayonnaise with mustard. Spread over salad, sealing edges carefully. Cover with plastic wrap and place in refrigerator. You may sprinkle with grated egg when ready to serve. This salad can stand for 2 or 3 days if not disturbed.

Do not stir or mix in mayonnaise. Just serve as is.

Hon. Mabel M. Deware, M.L.A.
Moncton West
New Brunswick

Caesar Salad

This universal favourite was contributed by 3 enthusiasts. Sheila Embury adds endive and 3-4 diced tomatoes to her salad, Ronald McNeil serves his minus the croutons.

2	small heads romaine lettuce		juice from ½ lemon
6	anchovies		small pinch dry mustard
1	large clove garlic, minced	2-3 drops	Tabasco
⅓ cup	olive oil	½ tsp.	salt
4 tsp.	vinegar	¼ tsp.	coarsely-ground black pepper
2 tsp.	Worcestershire sauce	¼ cup	Parmesan cheese
1	egg yolk		garlic croutons

Wash lettuce and wrap in paper towels. Chill in refrigerator. Rub anchovies and garlic in a wooden bowl around sides and bottom. Pour in olive oil to coat the inside of the bowl. Beat in the vinegar, Worcestershire, egg yolk, lemon juice, mustard, Tabasco sauce, salt, pepper and cheese. Add lettuce, croutons and toss.

Hon. Hugh Planche, M.L.A.
Calgary - Glenmore
Alberta
and
Mrs. Sheila Embury, M.L.A.
Calgary North West
Alberta

and
Ronald K. McNeil, M.P.P.
Elgin
Ontario

Onion Rings

This is excellent when served with Alberta Prime Roast of Beef or Barbecued Steak.

1	large Spanish onion	1 tsp.	celery seed
½ cup	sugar	⅓ cup	Miracle Whip
½ cup	white vinegar		

Slice Spanish onion into thin rings. Marinate overnight in sugar and vinegar. Before serving, drain, dry onion rings on paper towel Add celery seed and Miracle Whip.

Bob Porter, M.P.
Medicine Hat
Alberta

Long-Lasting Salad

1	head of cabbage, finely grated	1	large onion, thinly sliced
3 or 4	carrots, finely grated	¾ cup	sugar
			dressing

Mix vegetables together and sprinkle with sugar. Let sit 1 hour. Add dressing below. The salad can be kept in a covered container for up to 3 weeks.

Dressing:

1 cup	vinegar	¼ cup	sugar
2 tsp.	prepared mustard	1 tsp.	salt
3 tsp.	celery seed	¾ cup	vegetable oil

Bring first 5 ingredients to boil for 1 minutes. Add oil and bring back to boil. Immediately remove from heat. Cool and pour over salad.

Shirley Cripps, M.L.A.
Drayton Valley
Alberta

Cottage Cheese Salad

1 lb.	creamed cottage cheese	10 oz.	can oranges
3 oz.	pkg. orange Jell-o (85 g)	1	small carton Cool Whip
14 oz.	can crushed pineapple		

Combine cottage cheese and dry Jell-o crystals. Drain and add the pineapple and oranges. Fold in Cool Whip. Chill and serve.

Lloyd and Doreen Muller
L. J. Muller, M.L.A.
Shellbrook-Torch River
Saskatchewan

Ambrosia

This salad is a favourite from Newfoundland to Alberta. The Youngs add 1 cup of seedless grapes to their salad, in place of the maraschino cherries, while the Clarks use both.

2 x 10 oz.	tins mandarin oranges	2 cups	sour cream or dressing, below
2 x 14 oz.	tins pineapple chunks		
	maraschino cherries (for colour)	2 cups	miniature marshmallows
		2 cups	flaked coconut

Drain fruits well. Mix all ingredients together and let stand for several hours. This salad can be made 1 or 2 days ahead and will keep in the refrigerator for several days. It is a great favourite when served with turkey or ham.

Mary Clark substitutes a cooked dressing for the sour cream.

Dressing:

2	eggs	⅛ tsp.	salt
4 tbsp.	sugar	1 tbsp.	butter
4 tbsp.	vinegar	1 cup	cream, whipped

Combine eggs, sugar, vinegar and salt in double-boiler. Cook until thick. Add butter and cool. Fold in whipped cream gently. Add to fruit and marshmallow mixture. Chill 24 hours.

Eric, Jean, Lee Anne, Kira, Roland & Ben Berntson
Hon. E. A. Berntson, M.L.A.
Souris-Cannington
Saskatchewan
and
Hon. Haig Young, M.H.A.
Harbour Grace
Newfoundland and Labrador
and
Lewis and Mary Clark
Lewis Clark, M.L.A.
Drumheller
Alberta

Creamy Tomato Cucumber Salad

5	large tomatoes, coarsely chopped	¼ cup	chopped fresh parsley
1	large cucumber, thinly sliced	⅔ cup	sour cream
1 tsp.	salt	½ cup	hamburger relish
2	green onions, chopped	⅓ cup	mayonnaise
		1	clove garlic, minced

Combine tomatoes, cucumber and salt. Let stand 10 minutes, then drain well. Stir in green onions and parsley. Combine sour cream, relish, mayonnaise and garlic. Mix well. Stir into tomato mixture gently. Chill 1 to 2 hours before serving. Makes 6 servings.

David J. Carter, M.L.A.
Calgary Egmont
Alberta

Burn Bank Berry Salad

1 qt.	fresh Burn Bank strawberries	1 cup	whipping cream
¼ cup	sugar	2	bananas, peeled and sliced
2 x 3 oz.	pkgs. strawberry jelly powder (2 x 85 g)	2 cups	miniature marshmallows
			lettuce
3 cups	boiling water		whipped cream for garnish
14 oz.	can pineapple, well drained		Miracle Whip

Hull and wash strawberries. Reserve several for garnish. Slice remainder and sprinkle sugar on top. Prepare jelly as per package instructions, using juice from pineapple as part of the liquid to make 3 cups. Chill until partially set.

Whip cream and fold into jelly mixture. Carefully fold in the fruit and marshmallows and return to refrigerator until firm. We like a large flat pan for this salad, as it makes a large amount.

Cut into squares and serve on lettuce. Garnish with more whipped cream to which a small amount of Miracle Whip has been added. Top with reserved berries.
NOTE: This salad mixture is also an excellent dessert.

Lloyd and Isobel Hyde
Lloyd G. Hyde, M.L.A.
Portage la Prairie
Manitoba

Blushing Shrimp Salad

2 cups	tomato juice		4 oz.	can medium shrimp
3 oz.	pkg. cherry Jell-o (85 g)		½ cup	diced celery
½ tbsp.	vinegar		1 tbsp.	grated onion
			⅓ cup	grated carrot

Heat tomato juice and stir in Jell-o until dissolved. Add vinegar and chill. When partially set put in remaining ingredients. Serves 10 people.

Don and Lorraine Mazankowski
Hon. Don Mazankowski, P.C., M.P.
Vegreville
Alberta

Hot Seafood Salad

1 cup	canned shrimp, drained		1 tsp.	Worcestershire sauce
1 cup	canned crab meat, flaked		½ tsp.	salt
½ cup	finely chopped green onion		¼ tsp.	pepper
1 cup	finely chopped celery		½ cup	fine dry bread crumbs
¼ cup	minced onion		1 tbsp.	butter, melted
1 cup	mayonnaise			

Combine first 9 ingredients. Place in a 1½-quart greased casserole.

Combine bread crumbs with melted butter and sprinkle on top. Bake at 350°F for 25-30 minutes, or place in crab shells and bake 10-15 minutes. Delicious served with fresh vegetable salad. Serves 6.

John A. MacDougall, M.P.
Timiskaming
Ontario

Seafood Salad

2 cups	Creamette macaroni	1 bag	crushed potato chips
4	hard-boiled eggs		mayonnaise to moisten
1	tin, tuna, salmon OR shrimp	½ cup	cooked green peas, optional
½ cup	diced celery		

Cook macaroni in boiling salted water. Grate eggs. Drain tuna, salmon, or shrimp. Mix together cooled macaroni, eggs, the tuna, salmon, or shrimp, celery, and potato chips. Add enough mayonnaise to moisten. Green peas can be added if desired. Serves 4.

Hon. LeRoy Fjordbotten, M.L.A.
MacLeod
Alberta

Macaroni-Salmon Salad

¾ cup	elbow macaroni	2 tbsp.	finely chopped onion
1 tsp.	curry powder	7¾ oz.	can drained and flaked
1 cup	thinly sliced celery		salmon
1 cup	diced fresh apple	½ cup	mayonnaise

Cook macaroni and curry powder in a large amount of salted boiling water until macaroni is tender. Drain well, rinse and drain again. Cover and chill. Add celery, apple, onion and salmon to chilled macaroni and toss lightly, using 2 forks. Add mayonnaise and again toss salad lightly. Chill. Serves 4 or 5.

James E. Downey, M.L.A.
Arthur
Manitoba

Parsley and Egg Mayonnaise

This recipe is yummy and is a real breeze to make.

8	eggs, hard-boiled	⅔ cup	sour cream (small carton)
3	green onions		seasoning, as you wish
3 tbsp.	chopped fresh parsley		
⅔ cup	mayonnaise		

Slice hard-boiled eggs. Sprinkle with chopped green onion and 2 tbsp. parsley. Put in large flat dish for easy serving. Mix mayonnaise, sour cream and seasoning and pour over egg slices. Sprinkle with remaining onion and parsley. Chill. Great with cold meat, salad and crusty rolls — or whatever you fancy.

Robert and Vanessa Alexander
Robert Alexander, M.L.A.
Edmonton-Whitemud
Alberta

Lindenberg Relish

This no-cook relish recipe was handed down by Mrs. Miller's mother.

2	heads cabbage	½ cup	pickling salt
8	carrots	3 cups	sugar
12	good-sized onions	6 cups	vinegar
4	green peppers	1 tsp.	celery seed
4	red peppers	1 tsp.	mustard seed

Grind the fresh vegetables in a grinder. Cover with salt and let stand for 2 hours. Rinse vegetables in cold water and drain, then add remaining ingredients. Pack into sterilized jars and seal.

Bud and Margaret Miller
Hon. James E. "Bud" Miller, M.L.A.
Lloydminster
Alberta

Rhubarb Chutney

This is an original recipe from Prince Edward Island, given to us by friends. My family and I lived there for 9 happy years.

9 cups	(3 lb.) rhubarb		2 tsp.	cinnamon
9 cups	onions		2 tsp.	allspice
4 cups	dark vinegar		2 tsp.	cloves
1 cup	white sugar		2 tsp.	red pepper
2 tsp.	salt		7 cups	brown sugar

Prepare rhubarb by cutting into ½" pieces, put in blender until smooth. Prepare onions by cutting in small pieces and grating until smooth. Combine first 9 ingredients in large pot. Bring to boil, then cook slowly for 1 hour. Add brown sugar and cook until thick and smooth, 2 more hours. Ladle into jars and seal.

Eric K. Kipping, M.L.A.
Saint John North
New Brunswick

Autographs and Notes

Vegetables, Pasta and Rice

Mary Larson's Brussels Sprouts

4 cups	Brussels sprouts	¼ tsp.	paprika
1 cup	finely chopped onion		salt and white pepper to
¼ cup	butter		taste
2 cups	finely chopped celery	1 cup	diced Swiss cheese
3½ tbsp.	flour	⅔ cup	seasoned bread crumbs
1⅔ cup	scalded milk	3 tbsp.	chopped blanched almonds
½-¾ tsp.	nutmeg	2 tbsp.	butter

Seasoned Bread Crumbs

1 cup	dried bread crumbs	2 tsp.	oregano
4 tsp.	freshly grated Parmesan cheese		salt and pepper to taste

Cook sprouts until almost tender, 8 minutes. Cut in half. Sauté onion in butter until golden; stir in celery, cook 5 minutes. Stir in flour; cook 3 minutes. Remove from heat. Pour in scalded milk, stirring all the time. Return to heat; cook stirring until thick. Add nutmeg, paprika, salt and pepper. Fold in Brussels sprouts and Swiss cheese. Spoon into lightly buttered 2-quart baking dish. Combine ingredients for crumbs and sprinkle over top along with almonds. Dot with butter. Cook at 375°F for 20 minutes or until top is browned. Serves 8-10.

Hon. Barbara McDougall, P.C., M.P.
St. Paul
Ontario

Broccoli Casserole

1	bunch broccoli, parboiled	¼ cup	bread or cracker crumbs
10 oz.	can cream of chicken soup	¼ cup	grated Parmesan cheese
2 tbsp.	mayonnaise	2 tbsp.	melted butter
¼ cup	shredded cheese		

Cut broccoli into small pieces and place in 1-quart casserole. Combine soup, mayonnaise and cheese. Pour over broccoli. Mix crumbs, Parmesan, and melted butter. Sprinkle on top. Bake uncovered in 350°F oven for 40 minutes or until tender.

Hon. Gordon H. Dean, M.P.P.
Wentworth
Ontario

Broccoli Casserole

½ lb.	pkg. frozen chopped broccoli (Use fresh if available)	2 x 10 oz.	tins cream of mushroom soup
6 oz.	box Uncle Ben's Rice and Wild Rice Mixture (Better yet — 1½ cups of Saskatchewan Wild Rice if available)	1 lb.	jar Cheez Whiz
		10 oz.	can water chestnuts, sliced grated Cheddar cheese

Cook the broccoli until tender, then drain. Prepare rice. Mix everything together except the grated cheese. Sprinkle top with cheese. Bake in 350°F oven for 1 hour. This recipe can be prepared ahead of time. Serves 10-12.

Hon. Jack Klein, M.L.A.
Minister of Tourism and Small Business
Regina North
Saskatchewan

Broccoli Casserole

1	clove of garlic, minced	10 oz.	can cream of mushroom soup
1	large onion, chopped		
¼ cup	butter	7 oz.	roll sharp cheese snack OR 7 oz. Cheese Whiz
4 cups	bite-sized broccoli pieces		
10 oz.	can sliced mushrooms, drained OR fresh mushrooms (sauté with onion)	¼ cup	chopped almonds
		½ cup	buttered bread crumbs

Sauté onion and garlic in butter. Spoon into large, greased casserole. Cook broccoli until crunchy. Add to casserole. Add mushrooms and chopped almonds. In a separate bowl, blend mushroom soup and cheese. Fold into casserole. Top with almonds and buttered bread crumbs. Bake at 350°F for 45 minutes. Serves 10.

Joan and Harvie Andre
Hon. Harvie Andre, P.C., M.P.
Calgary Centre
Alberta

Perogy Dough

3 cups	mashed potatoes (do not add milk)	1 tsp.	salt
4 cups	flour	2	eggs
		½ cup	Mazola oil

Blend mashed potatoes into flour and salt, like you would for pastry. Then add eggs and oil. Knead dough. Cover dough and let rise 10 minutes or more. Roll out and cut into 2" circles. Put filling into centre and fold dough over forming ½ circle, pressing edges together. Boil in hot water until they rise, plus 3-4 minutes.

Serve with cream and onions or sour cream or with melted butter and onions and bacon bits.

Hon. Peter Trynchy, M.L.A.
Whitecourt
Alberta

Leones

| 10 cups | mashed potatoes | 1 cup | margarine |
| 6 tbsp. | cream | 4 cups | flour |

Mix together mashed potatoes, cream, and margarine. Cool and add flour. Roll out like pie crust. Fry in a hot flat pan on both sides. Wrap in a towel to cool. Fold and cut. Serve with butter and sugar.

Larry and Beryl Birkbeck
L. W. Birkbeck, M.L.A.
Moosomin
Saskatchewan

Creamy Hash Brown Bake

10 oz.	can condensed cream of celery soup	4 cups	frozen hash brown potatoes
⅓ cup	milk	1	small onion, chopped
4 oz.	pkg. cream cheese	½ cup	shredded sharp process cheese

In a saucepan combine soup, milk and cream cheese. Cook and stir until smooth. Add potatoes and onion. Pour into 10" x 6" x 1½" pan. Cover with foil and bake at 350°F for 1¼ hours. Top with grated cheese, return to oven until cheese melts.

Hon. Charles Mayer, P.C., M.P.
Portage-Marquette
Manitoba

Potatoes Deluxe

32 oz.	pkg. frozen hash browns, thawed	½ cup	butter or margarine, melted
		1½ tsp.	salt
10 oz.	cream of chicken soup	1	med. onion, diced
1 cup	sour cream	2 cups	crushed cornflakes
2 cups	shredded Cheddar cheese (8 oz.)	¼ cup	melted margarine

Grease a 13" x 9" baking dish. Preheat oven 350°F. Combine all ingredients except cornflakes and margarine. Spoon into baking dish. In a small bowl, combine cornflakes and margarine, sprinkle over potatoes. Bake 45 minutes or until bubbly. Makes 12 servings.

Hazel and Frank Johnston
J. Frank Johnston, M.L.A.
Sturgeon Creek
Manitoba

Irish Potato Cakes

2 cups	well-mashed potatoes	2 cups	flour
1 tsp.	salt		

Mix all ingredients well and turn out on a well-floured board. Knead well, until it feels like very stiff dough. More or less flour may be used. Roll very thin; cut in shapes with knife. Fry in a pan as you would for pancakes. Delicious served with bacon or sausages.

Bill and Bev McKnight
Hon. Bill McKnight, P.C., M.P.
Kindersley-Lloydminster
Saskatchewan

Make-Ahead Turnips

This was the only way my mother could convince me, as a child, that turnips were good for me and good to eat! I used the same trick on my children with the same success! Hopefully, a new generation of our family will find the same delights in TURNIPS that the last four have.

2-3	medium turnips	3 tsp.	salt
1 cup	applesauce OR 2 chopped apples	¼ tsp.	black pepper
		2	eggs
6 tbsp.	butter OR margarine	1¾ cups	soft bread crumbs
4 tsp.	sugar	2 tbsp.	melted butter OR margarine

Cook peeled, cubed turnips in salted water and drain. Mash well and combine all ingredients except half of the bread crumbs and the two tablespoons of melted butter. Mix well. Pour into a greased 2-quart casserole. Toss remaining bread crumbs with melted butter and sprinke over turnip dish. Cool slightly, cover and refrigerate. Remove 1 hour before dinner, heat uncovered in 350°F oven for approximately 30 minutes.

Serves 8-10 people. It can be made 3 days ahead. Applesauce or apples can be substituted with other fruits such as peaches, pineapple.

When my children were young, I used the leftovers for a turnip and meat pie the next day. I found it economical, time-saving and good.

Hon. P. A. Smith, M.L.A.
Swift Current
Saskatchewan

Squash Casserole

1	medium squash (approximately 4 cups cooked)	1 cup	cream of chicken soup
		1 cup	sour cream
		1 box	MacLaren's stuffing
1	small onion, chopped	1 cup	butter or margarine, melted
1 cup	raw shredded carrot		

Cook, drain and mash the squash. Mix in the onion, carrot, soup and sour cream. Mix the box of MacLaren's stuffing with the butter. Put ½ the mixture in the bottom of a casserole and put the squash mixture on top of it. Add the remaining stuffing on top. Bake for 40 minutes at 350°F.

Malcolm and Hazel MacLeod
Hon. Malcolm MacLeod, M.L.A.
Albert
New Brunswick

Sweet Potato Supreme

This recipe is a pleasant change from rice or potatoes.

2 cups	mashed, cooked sweet potatoes	¼ tsp.	paprika
		½ cup	packed brown sugar
2 tbsp.	cream or milk	½ cup	butter
2 tbsp.	melted butter scant tsp. salt	1 cup	(approximately) pecan halves

Thoroughly mix potatoes, cream, butter, salt and paprika. Spread in greased casserole. Make the topping by heating brown sugar and butter over low heat, stirring constantly, until butter is barely melted. It is important not to cook after butter is melted, or the topping will harden when casserole is heated. Spread topping over potatoes and cover with pecan halves. Refrigerate until ready to heat. This casserole may be warmed in an oven of any temperature or microwave, but should be bubbling hot before serving.

Hon. Nancy Teed, M.L.A.
Saint John South
New Brunswick

Zippy Glazed Carrots

3 cups	sliced carrots	2 tbsp.	prepared mustard
2 tbsp.	butter or margarine	¼ tsp.	salt
¼ cup	brown sugar	1 tbsp.	snipped parsley

Cook and drain carrots. Melt butter in skillet. Stir in brown sugar, mustard and salt. Add cooked carrots; heat, stirring constantly, until carrots are nicely glazed, about 5 minutes. Sprinkle with parsley. Serves 4.

Lorne McCuish, M.P.
Prince George-Bulkley Valley
British Columbia

Brunswick Stew

This is meatless and made with fresh vegetables* from our garden. It has been a prized recipe in our family for many years. In July and August, this is a very special (and nutritious!) treat for our friends and relatives at our "farm" in Springfield, N.B. Amounts vary as to how many you are serving.

new potatoes, (golf ball size)	peas, very young
new string beans, green, yellow OR both	celery
	green pepper
new small onions	cereal cream
new cauliflower florets	butter
new broccoli florets	salt and pepper

*You can use any fresh vegetables available.

Place vegetables in large pot with about ½" of water and salt to taste. Bring to a boil, cook until tender, not too soft. Remove from heat. Do not drain off any liquid. Add cereal cream to cover as for soup, a large piece of butter, and salt and pepper to taste. Reheat but do not boil.

Delicious during the garden season.

Hon. Gerald S. Merrithew, P.C., M.P.
St. John
New Brunswick

Celery Casserole

4 cups	diced celery	10 oz.	can whole mushrooms
¼ cup	slivered almonds	10 oz.	can cream of chicken soup
½ cup	water chestnuts	¼ cup	Parmesan cheese
		½ cup	bread crumbs

Mix first 5 ingredients together with a spoon. Sprinkle the top with cheese and crumbs. Cook at 350°F for 40 minutes.

Murray Dorin and Karen Lynch
Murray Dorin, M.P.
Edmonton West
Alberta

Green Bean Casserole

This recipe you can make ahead — heat just before dinner. Serves 8. Delicious!

2 x 12 oz.	pkg. frozen French-cut green beans	1 cup	creammilk
		1½ cups	grated sharp Cheddar cheese
1	medium onion, diced	½ tsp.	Tabasco sauce
10 oz.	can mushroom stems and pieces	1 tsp.	salt
		½ tsp.	pepper
½ cup	margarine	5 oz.	tin water chestnuts, drained and sliced
½ cup	flour		
2 cups	milk	½ cup	toasted, slivered almonds

Cook and drain green beans. Sauté onion and mushrooms in margarine. Add flour and mix. Add milk and cream; stir until thickened. Add remaining ingredients, except beans, water chestnuts and almonds, and simmer until cheese melts. Add cooked green beans and water chestnuts and mix well. Pour into greased shallow casserole. Sprinkle with slivered almonds. Bake at 350°F for 35 to 40 minutes.

Grant and Sheron Schmidt
G. J. Schmidt, M.L.A.
Melville
Saskatchewan

Beans, Beans, Beans

14 oz.	can seasoned green beans French-cut	1	green pepper, chopped
14 oz.	can kidney beans	1	onion, chopped
2 x 14 oz.	cans pork and beans	½ lb.	bacon, cut in pieces
14 oz.	can lima beans	1 cup	brown sugar
		16 oz.	bottle chili sauce

Drain beans; add some of the liquid later if needed. Sauté green pepper and onion with chopped bacon. Combine brown sugar with chili sauce. Mix all ingredients together in a crock pot and cook slowly all day, or in oven for 1½ hours at 300°F. Stir often. This serves about 20 people and is great to serve with barbecued hamburgers.

Bob and Phyllis Larter
R. A. (Bob) Larter
Agent General in the United Kingdom for Saskatchewan
London, England

Scotchish Baked Beans

2 cups	soldier (navy) beans	¼ lb.	salt pork (OR bacon OR ¼ cup vegetable oil OR 4 pork sausages)
1	medium onion, quartered		
3 tbsp.	maple syrup		
2 tbsp.	ketchup	1 tbsp.	salt
2 tbsp.	dry mustard	1 cup	Scotch whiskey, borrowed

Soak beans overnight. Next day add more water, if needed, to cover beans, bring to a boil and simmer for a half hour or more, or until tender. Drain beans, reserving the water, and add to beans the remaining ingredients. Put in bean pot, cover with reserved water. Bake, covered for at least 6 hours in 250°F oven keeping the beans covered with water.

You may add the following to this recipe if you approve. I call this "Scotchish Baked Beans". (Of course the alcohol is cooked out and only the peat flavour remains.) Borrow 1 cup of Scotch whiskey. A half hour before removing the beans from the oven, uncover the crock and add the Scotch whiskey. Bake for the last half hour.

Hon. Richard Hatfield, P.C., M.L.A.
Premier of New Brunswick

Baked Beans

2 lbs.	white beans	½ cup	brown sugar
1 tsp.	baking soda	2 tsp.	mustard
1 lb.	bacon	3 tsp.	salt
1	medium onion	½ tsp.	pepper
⅔ cup	molasses		

Soak beans overnight. Drain and parboil for 20 minutes with 1 tsp. baking soda. Rinse in cold water. Put ½ of bacon and onion in bean pot. Add beans and remaining bacon. Mix molasses and dry ingredients with hot water, adding to beans to cover. Stir every hour. Bake at 300°F for 6 hours.

Murray and Betty Cardiff
Murray Cardiff, M.P.
Huron - Bruce
Ontario

Boston Baked Beans

As a boy in Prince Edward Island I grew fond of the beans which were a traditional Saturday supper dish. Whatever was left in the crock became the pièce de résistance of Sunday's breakfast. Like stew, beans are best warmed over.

3 cups	yellow-eyed, kidney or pinto beans, soaked overnight	¼ cup	molasses (I prefer ½ cup molasses and omit the brown sugar)
½ lb.	salt pork, OR bacon		
1 tbsp.	dry mustard	1 cup	water
¼ cup	dark brown sugar	1	large onion, sliced seasonings

Boil beans a half hour. Place in bean pot in layers alternating with salt pork. Add the mustard, sugar, molasses, water, onion and a shake of ginger and other favourite but restrained seasonings if desired. Some people may like to add 1 tsp. salt although they would be better off without it. Bake in a slow oven, 225°F 6-8 hours. I like to place some split sausages on top about 2 hours before beans are baked.

Hon. Heath Macquarrie
The Senate
Prince Edward Island

Kutia

This is the first dish served on Ukrainian Christmas Eve.

1 cup	wheat	1½ tbsp.	poppy seeds, ground
	honey		

Select nice clean kernels of wheat. Soak overnight. Drain. Put to boil over medium heat. Stir often. When water boils out put more in. Cook 4 hours until kernels are fluffy and some split. When cooked, add honey according to taste. Add crushed poppy seeds. Mix well. If you can't grind poppy seeds, boil in milk for about 20 minutes. When it boils out and seeds are softened, add to wheat. Serve in fruit dishes. Serves 6.

Jo-Ann Zazelenchuk, M.L.A.
Saskatoon Riversdale
Saskatchewan

Scanterbury Casserole

First encountered in Pine Falls, Manitoba, this recipe has become a family favourite.

6	strips bacon	10 oz.	can mushrooms
2	onions, chopped	2 tbsp.	butter
1	green pepper, chopped		salt and pepper
3	stalks celery, chopped	¼ lb.	Manitoba wild rice (about 1 cup)

Fry bacon until crisp. Remove. Fry onions, pepper, celery, mushrooms in butter. Add salt and pepper. Rinse rice with cold water. Cover with water to a depth of 1". Boil until kernels begin to split and most of water is absorbed. Mix rice and vegetables. Put in casserole and bake in oven for 1½ hours. (Optional: Add several teaspoons soy sauce). Add beef broth or water if casserole is dry while baking.

Serve with Cornish hen (1½ hours for chicken to bake), cranberries in orange halves, and broccoli and cauliflower baked with cheese sauce.

Hon. Jake Epp, M.P.
Provencher
Manitoba

Sunflower Roast

1 cup	shelled sunflower seeds	2 tsp.	mixed seasonings (your choice; suggest mixture of sage, savory, celery salt, marjoram, thyme, salt)
½ cup	chopped walnuts		
1½ cups	cooked brown rice		
1 cup	cooked Caribou Brand wild rice (from LaRonge Industries)	¹⁄₁₆ tsp.	garlic powder
½ cup	finely chopped onion		

Grind sunflower seeds in coffee grinder. Mix all ingredients together. Place into lightly buttered casserole dish. Cover and bake 45 minutes at 350°F.

Hon. Jack Sandberg, M.L.A.
Saskatoon Centre
Saskatchewan

Brown Rice

This Brown Rice dish is delicious. Serve with everything from ham to chicken.

½ cup	butter	½ cup	chopped or grated carrots
1 cup	white rice	½ cup	finely chopped celery
1 cup	finely chopped onion	½ cup	snipped parsley
	salt to taste	10 oz.	can sliced mushrooms
2 x 10 oz.	cans beef consommé		

Melt butter in deep skillet. Add white rice, onion and salt. Let brown until the color of golden wheat. Put in casserole. Add beef consommé. Bake 45 minutes in 350°F oven. Then add carrots, celery, parsley and mushrooms. Cook 20 minutes longer. This can be made ahead and frozen.

Ted, Kate, Meghan and Simon Schellenberg
Ted Schellenberg, M.P.
Nanaimo-Alberni
British Columbia

Gourmet Wild Rice and Cheese Casserole

1 cup	wild rice	½ cup	butter
3 cups	boiling water	1 cup	grated old Cheddar cheese
¼ tsp.	salt	19 oz.	can tomatoes
½ lb.	mushrooms, sliced (about 3 cups)	1 tsp.	salt
		1 cup	hot water
½ cup	chopped onion		

Cook rice, uncovered in boiling salted water until nearly tender, about 30 minutes. Drain rice if necessary. Sauté mushrooms and onion in butter for about 5 minutes. Toss rice with all ingredients. Place in buttered 2-quart casserole. cover and bake 1 hour at 350°F. Makes 6¼ cups or 6-8 servings.
NOTE: This may be prepared the day before and baked just before serving. Serve as a vegetable with pork, poultry or game.

Hon. Peter Lougheed, P.C., M.L.A.
Premier of Alberta

Wild Rice Amandine en Casserole

2 cups	wild rice	3 tbsp.	chopped green pepper
½ cup	butter	4½ cups	hot chicken broth
2 tbsp.	chopped onion		salt and pepper
2 tbsp.	chives	¾ cup	shredded almonds
1 tsp.	chopped shallots		

Wash and drain wild rice. Heat butter and stir in onions, chives, shallots, and green pepper. Stir the mixture into the rice and cook over a very gentle heat, stirring constantly, until the rice begins to turn yellow. Stir in chicken broth. Season to taste with salt and pepper and add almonds. Turn the mixture into a casserole and bake, covered, in a slow oven, 325°F, for 1¼ hours, or until rice is tender. Serves 10.

Hon. Leo Bernier, M.P.P.
Kenora
Ontario

Noodles All'Alfredo

12 oz.	pkg. broad noodles	¼ tsp.	salt
½ cup	butter	dash	pepper
1 cup	cream	2 tbsp.	chopped fresh parsley
1 cup	grated Parmesan cheese		

Cook noodles in large amount of boiling salted water. Drain. Return to pan. In small saucepan, combine butter and cream. Heat until butter melts. Add ¾ cup Parmesan cheese, salt and pepper. Simmer 1-2 minutes. Combine sauce and parsley with noodles. Sprinkle with remaining Parmesan cheese. Serve with bottle of good Canadian Wine. (Niagara Wines are our favourites!)

Rob Nicholson, M.P.
Niagara Falls
Ontario

Noodle Kugel

12 oz.	pkg. medium noodles	salt and pepper to taste
4-5	eggs	ground onion to taste
		(optional)

Cook noodles in boiling salted water. Drain. Beat eggs in blender or mixer, add salt and pepper and sautéed onions. Add eggs to noodles and mix well. Pour into a greased casserole dish, or 9" x 9" cake pan, which has been preheated. Bake at 400°F for 40-50 minutes or longer if desired. This dish goes well with chicken, beef or meatballs as a main course, or as a snack.

Ralph Katzman, M.L.A.
Rosthern
Saskatchewan

Autographs and Notes

Entrées

Favourite Oven-Fried Chicken

½ cup	butter	3 tsp.	paprika
1 cup	flour	1	fryer chicken, OR 8 chicken
2 tsp.	salt		breasts
¼ tsp.	pepper		

Pre-heat oven to 400°F, and have oven rack on top or 2nd setting in oven. Melt the butter on a shallow baking pan or cookie sheet. Remove from oven as soon as melted. Place flour in plastic bag, and salt, pepper and paprika. Shake well to mix. Dip chicken pieces in this mixture. As each piece of chicken is coated, place on pan, turn and coat all sides with butter, then turn to bake, skin side down. Bake on one side 30 minutes, then turn and bake another 30 minutes. This results in a nicely browned, tasty chicken.

Optional: This barbecue sauce may be served separately, in a condiment dish at table, or for those who like barbecued fowl, pour over chicken the last 15 minutes of baking.

Barbecue Sauce:

½ cup	sliced onion	½ tsp.	chili powder
1 tsp.	salt	1¼ tsp.	black pepper
1 tbsp.	vinegar	½ cup	ketchup
1 tbsp.	sugar	¼ cup	water
1 tbsp.	Worcestershire sauce		

Combine all ingredients in saucepan and simmer 15 minutes.

Grant Hodgins, M.L.A.
Melfort
Saskatchewan

Apricot Chicken

8 oz.	bottle French dressing	½ cup	water
1	small jar apricot jam	2	small frying chickens
1 pkg.	onion soup mix		

Mix above ingredients together and pour over cut-up chicken. Bake in 375°F oven until chicken is tender, about 1½ hours.

Keith Parker, M.L.A.
Moose Jaw-North
Saskatchewan

Okanagan Peach Chicken

1	cut-up chicken OR 4 chicken breasts, split	½ cup	barbecue sauce
		½ cup	chopped onions
¼ cup	flour	2 tbsp.	soy sauce
¼ tsp.	salt	6 oz.	can water chestnuts, drained and sliced
	dash pepper		
	cooking oil	1	green pepper, cut in strips
20 oz.	can peaches		

Coat chicken with seasoned flour. Brown well in small amount of oil. Drain. Combine peaches, barbecue sauce, onion and soy sauce. Pour over chicken. Cover and simmer 40 minutes or until chicken is tender. Add green pepper and water chestnuts for last 10 minutes of cooking. Serve with rice. 6-8 servings.

Fred King, M.P.
Okanagan-Similkameen
British Columbia

Pineapple Ginger Chicken

2½-3 lb.	broiler fryer, cut up	2 tbsp.	liquid honey
	salt and pepper	1 tbsp.	chopped candied ginger
½ cup	butter	dash	pepper sauce
4 tsp.	flour		hot cooked rice
½ cup	barbecue sauce		parsley, chopped
19 oz.	can chunk pineapple		

Season chicken with salt and pepper, brown in butter. Drain off excess fat. Gradually add flour to barbecue sauce mixing until well blended. Drain pineapple reserving juice; add juice, honey, ginger and pepper sauce to barbecue sauce mixture. Pour over chicken. Cover and simmer 40 minutes or until chicken is tender. Alternatively place chicken in casserole, cover and bake in 350°F oven 35-40 minutes. Place chicken over rice and sprinkle with parsley. Serves 4-6.

W. F. Purdy, M.L.A.
Stony Plain Constituency
Alberta

Sweet and Sour Chicken

5-6 lbs.	cut-up chicken	1 cup	water
1 cup	ketchup	1 tbsp.	onion salt OR powder
¼ cup	chili sauce	1 tsp.	Worcestershire sauce
½ cup	brown sugar	2 tbsp.	lemon juice OR juice of 1
1 tsp.	garlic powder OR garlic salt		lemon

Broil both sides of chicken until brown. Place in roaster and cover with sauce made from remaining ingredients. Bake in oven at 350°F for 1 hour.

John A. Newell, M.L.A.
Cape Breton the Lakes
Nova Scotia

Chicken Curry

From scratch — Except the chicken. It's a great curry dish — but not for the faint of heart! If you are really serious eat it with your fingers!

4	cloves garlic, crushed	5 lbs.	chicken
2 tbsp.	coriander	1	onion, sliced
2 tsp.	turmeric		corn oil
2 tsp.	cumin	2 cups	water
½ tsp.	crushed mustard seed	2	tomatoes, halved
½ tsp.	ginger	3	cinnamon sticks
1 tsp.	crushed red pepper	1 cup	raw rice
3	whole cardamoms, crushed		

Mix garlic, coriander, turmeric, cumin, mustard seed, ginger, red pepper, and cardamom into a powder. Cut up and bone (or not) chicken. Mix powder well into chicken parts. Sauté sliced onion in a very little corn oil in large pot until lightly browned. Add chicken and simmer until meat has whitened.

Add water, tomato halves and cinnamon. Cook slowly until broth is just below boil and give it some extra time for good measure.

Use broth to cook rice (1 cup) and mix in with chicken.

Serve with papard and a buttermilk, tomato, cucumber, mustard seed side dish.

R. A. Corbett, M.P.
Fundy-Royal
New Brunswick

Lemon Pepper Chicken

An easy and delicious barbecue recipe for the hot summer. This is an easy meal to prepare with little clean-up.

6	chicken breasts	4 tbsp.	soy sauce per breast
1	whole lemon, cut into 6 pieces		whole black peppercorns

Place each breast in a double layer of foil. On each squeeze 1 section of lemon, drizzle with 4 tbsp. of soy sauce and sprinkle with coarsely ground pepper. Fold the foil and seal. Do not invert as the soy sauce will leak out. Place in the oven or on the barbecue with the lid down. Bake at 350°F, in either unit, for 15-30 minutes, depending on the size of the breasts. Serve with baked potatoes and a vegetable done on the barbecue.

Peter Duguay and Charlette James Duguay
Leo Duguay, M.P.
St. Boniface
Manitoba

Curried Chicken

2	large onions, finely chopped	¼ tsp.	cinnamon
2 oz.	butter and 2 tsps. olive OR corn oil	2 tbsp.	sweet pickle OR chutney
		1 tbsp.	lemon juice
1	garlic clove, finely chopped	3 tsp.	sugar
2 tbsp.	curry powder	1 cup	stock OR water
1 tbsp.	flour	½-1 tsp.	salt
2	whole cloves	1	medium-sized chicken (I use just chicken breasts)
1 tbsp.	tomato paste		
¼ tsp.	ginger		

Sauté onion in butter and oil until clear. Combine all ingredients and pour over chicken breasts in baking dish. Bake at 250-300°F for 3-4 hours.

Halvar and Maxine Jonson
Halvar C. Jonson, M.L.A.
Ponoka-Rimbey
Alberta

Curried Chicken

5	chicken breasts	½ cup	chopped onion
2-3 cups	water	1	carrot, cut up

Sauce:

2	onions, chopped	2 x 10 oz.	tins chicken broth
1	green pepper, chopped	2 tbsp.	soy sauce
2	apples, diced	2 tbsp.	tomato paste
2	celery stalks, chopped		juice of ½ lemon
2	carrots, chopped	3 tbsp.	brown sugar
2 tbsp.	oil	½ cup	raisins
2 tsp.	curry powder	10 oz.	tin mushrooms
10 oz.	tin cream of chicken soup	1 tbsp.	cornstarch

Boil the first 4 ingredients for 10 minutes, until chicken is tender and then cool. Keep liquid and put chicken in refrigerator until cool and then cube. Meanwhile, prepare sauce.

Sauté chopped onion, green pepper, apple, celery, and carrot. Put in oil, then add 2 tsp. curry powder and stir. Add soup, chicken broth, and soy sauce to tomato paste, lemon juice, brown sugar, raisins and mushrooms; simmer for 1½ hours until thick. Add cornstarch if not thick enough. Add chicken breasts, simmer an additional ½ hour. Serve with rice or potatoes.

John McLennon, M.H.A.
Windsor-Buchans
Newfoundland and Labrador

Glorifried Chicken

4	chicken breasts (OR other chicken parts)	1 tsp.	paprika
		⅛ tsp.	pepper
⅓ cup	flour	10 oz.	can cream of chicken soup
1 tsp.	salt	1	soup can water

Coat chicken, 1 piece at a time with mixture of flour and spices. Heat vegetable oil in skillet. Brown chicken pieces on all sides.

Place in casserole dish. Cover with chicken soup mixed with 1 can of water.

Bake, covered, at 350°F for 45 minutes, then uncover for another 15 minutes.

Bob Myers, M.L.A.
Saskatoon South
Saskatchewan

Chicken and Broccoli

4	whole chicken breasts	¼ tsp.	curry powder
1	onion, sliced	2 x 10 oz.	pkgs. frozen broccoli spears
2 x 10 oz.	cans cream of chicken soup		OR 2 bunches fresh
	(3 cans if you wish)		broccoli
¾ cup	mayonnaise		grated Cheddar cheese
1 tsp.	lemon juice		well-buttered bread crumbs

Poach chicken in salted water with sliced onion. Skin and bone. Mix together soup, mayonnaise, lemon juice and curry powder. Cook broccoli, drain well and arrange in 13" x 9" baking dish. Cover with chicken. Pour soup mixture over chicken and cover it with the cheese and then a thick layer of crumbs. Bake 30-40 minutes at 350°F. Serves 8. Can be prepared in advance. Also, it freezes well.

Jim and Sheila Edwards
Jim Edwards, M.P.
Edmonton South
Alberta
and

Ken and Mary Ellen James
Ken James, M.P.
Sarnia-Lambton
Ontario

Romanian Chicken

This recipe was passed on to me by my grandmother, who came from the Ukraine.

3 lbs.	chicken, cut up	dash	hot pepper sauce
	flour	10 oz.	can condensed tomato soup
2 tbsp.	shortening	1 cup	water
1	medium onion, sliced	½ cup	celery diced
1	large clove of garlic, minced	2 oz.	natural Swiss cheese,
1 tsp.	salt		shredded
½ tsp.	dried basil	½ cup	hot, buttered noodles

Coat chicken lightly with flour. In skillet, brown chicken in hot shortening. Combine onion, garlic, salt, basil, hot pepper sauce, tomato soup and water. Pour over chicken. Simmer, covered for 40 minutes. Add celery and cook 10 to 15 minutes longer or until tender. Stir in ¼ cup of cheese. Sprinkle remaining cheese on top. Serve with hot, buttered noodles. Serves 4.

Evelyn Bacon, M.L.A.
Saskatoon-Nutana
Saskatchewan

Chicken à la King

1	large leek, white and pale green part only, sliced	1 cup	cream (half 'n half)
½ cup	celery	2	chicken bouillon cubes dissolved in ⅓ cup boiling water
¼ cup	chopped green pepper		white pepper
1 cup	sliced fresh mushrooms		salt
2-3 tbsp.	margarine	3 cups	diced cooked chicken
⅓ cup	margarine	¼ cup	chopped pimiento
⅓ cup	flour		
2 cups	chicken broth		

Sauté leeks, celery, green pepper and mushrooms in 2-3 tablespoons margarine. Do not allow vegetables to burn or become too soft. Remove from pan, add the ⅓ cup margarine and flour. Blend, cook over low heat a few minutes. Remove from heat, slowly stir in broth, cream and dissolved bouillon cubes. Bring to boil, stirring, over medium low heat. Boil 1 minute, add seasonings. Reduce heat, add chicken, vegetables, pimiento, cook until meat is heated through. Serve over rice, hot biscuits or shells. Serves 6.

Hon. Sterling Lyon, P.C., M.L.A.
Charleswood
Manitoba

Chicken Newburg

⅓ cup	butter	1 tsp.	minced onion
¼ cup	flour	¼ tsp.	pepper
2 cups	milk	½ cup	sliced mushrooms, sautéed
¾ cup	shredded Cheddar cheese	½ cup	slivered toasted almonds
1 tbsp.	chopped pimiento	1½ cups	cubed cooked chicken
1 tsp.	salt	¼ cup	cooking sherry

Melt butter, add the flour, blending well. Then add the milk, stirring constantly, and cook over low heat until sauce is smooth and has thickened. Add cheese, stir until melted into sauce. Add pimiento, salt, onion, pepper, mushrooms, almonds, chicken and sherry. Serve hot over patty shells. Serves about 6.

Horace Carver, M.L.A.
Third Queen's
Prince Edward Island

Chicken/Lobster Bake

6	chicken breasts	¼-½ cup	milk
10 oz.	can Highliner cream of		garlic powder
	lobster soup	1 cup	grated Cheddar cheese
			green onions

Bone chicken breasts if desired. Place chicken pieces in greased baking dish. Dilute soup with some of the milk. Sprinkle chicken with garlic powder. Cover pieces with diluted soup. Cover soup mixture with cheese. Bake at 350°F for 45 minutes, uncovered. Before serving, sprinkle with finely chopped green onions.

William C. Attewell, M.P.
Don Valley East
Ontario

Chicken Parmesan

3 tsp.	oil	⅛ tsp.	salt
½ cup	onion	⅛ tsp.	pepper
1	clove garlic	1 lb.	boneless chicken breasts
16 oz.	can tomatoes, drained	¼ cup	seasoned crumbs
1 tbsp.	tomato paste		Parmesan cheese
⅛ tsp.	oregano	3 oz.	mozzarella cheese, shredded
⅛ tsp.	basil		

Heat 1 tsp. oil over medium heat, sauté onion and garlic 5 minutes, add tomatoes, breaking up with fork, tomato paste and spices. Simmer uncovered 10 minutes until thick. Heat oven to 375°F. Pound chicken until thin. Mix equal amounts of crumbs and Parmesan, dip chicken to coat, fry chicken in remaining oil until browned. Place cutlets in shallow 11" x 7" pan and cover with sauce. Sprinkle with mozzarella cheese and additional Parmesan. Bake 15 minutes until cheese is melted. Serves 4.

J. Barry Turner, M.P.
Ottawa-Carleton
Ontario

Chicken in Parmesan Cream

6	chicken breasts, skinned and boned	1 cup	light cream (table OR half and half)
	salt and pepper to taste	½ cup	grated Parmesan cheese
5 tbsp.	butter	3	egg yolks, beaten
2 tbsp.	flour	½ cup	bread crumbs

Season chicken with salt and pepper. In frying pan melt half the butter and cook chicken until brown on both sides. Partially cover pan and cook until tender, about 30 minutes. Preheat oven to 350°F.

In saucepan melt remaining butter, add the flour and stir with wire whisk until blended. Add cream and beat until thickened and smooth. You may have to add more cream. Stir in 1 tbsp. of cheese and beaten egg yolks. Stir until smooth.

Sprinkle ½ remaining cheese in bottom of 9" x 13" pan. Lay chicken pieces on top. Cover with sauce. Bake for 20 minutes until heated throughout. Mix remaining cheese with bread crumbs and sprinkle on top. Broil until golden brown.

Bob Brisco, M.P.
Kootenay West
British Columbia

Chicken Suisse

4	chicken breasts, boned and skinned	10 oz.	can mushroom soup
¼ cup	butter	¾ cup	dry sherry
½ cup	chopped onions	1 tbsp.	chopped parsley
1 cup	sliced peeled mushrooms	1 tsp.	salt
		2	lemon slices

Brown chicken in ¼ cup butter and put in casserole. Add onions and mushrooms to pan and cook until tender but not brown. Add soup, sherry, parsley, salt and paprika. Blend well. Pour mixture over chicken and place 2 lemon slices on top. Bake uncovered at 325°F degrees for 1 hour.

Paul and Judy Dick
Paul Dick, Q.C., M.P.
Lanark - Renfrew - Carleton
Ontario

Chicken Breasts in Sour Cream and Paprika

6	whole chicken breasts, boned and skinned	4	cloves garlic, minced
2 cups	sour cream	4 tsp.	salt
¼ cup	lemon juice	½ tsp.	pepper
4 tsp.	Worcestershire sauce	1½ cups	fine bread crumbs
2 tsp.	paprika	¾ cup	butter

Put all ingredients in bowl except crumbs and butter. Cover and refrigerate overnight. Coat chicken in crumbs. Arrange in shallow baking dish and pour over half the melted butter. Bake at 350°F for 45 minutes. Add remaining butter and bake 15 minutes longer. Serve with rice.

David and Mary Daubney
David Daubney, M.P.
Ottawa West
Ontario

Boned Stuffed Chicken Breasts

2	skinned and boned chicken breasts	1 cup	cooked frozen French-style green beans
dash	each pepper, garlic powder and paprika	1 cup	tomato sauce OR purée oregano
8	slices Swiss cheese		cooked spaghetti

Pound chicken breasts to ⅛" thickness. Cut each breast in half and season with pepper, garlic powder and paprika. Place a slice of Swiss cheese and ¼ of the green beans on each piece of chicken; roll to enclose filling. Place rolls in baking pan, seam side down. Pour tomato sauce evenly over stuffed chicken breasts and sprinkle with oregano. Top each roll with a slice of cheese. Bake at 350°F for 25 minutes. Serve the stuffed rolls and sauce over hot spaghetti. Serves 2.

Morrissey and Betty Ann Johnson
Morrissey Johnson, M.P.
Bonavista-Trinity-Conception
Newfoundland and Labrador

Hungarian Paprikás Csirke (Paprika Chicken)

3 lb.	frying chicken, disjointed	1 tsp.	salt
2	onions, finely chopped	1 cup	cream
3 tbsp.	oil		soft noodles
1 tbsp.	paprika		

Wash chicken well and drain. Brown the onions lightly in the oil; add the paprika and the chicken. Sprinkle with salt. Use enough water just to cover and cook slowly about 1 hour or until tender. Pour the cream over the chicken. Heat for 1 or 2 minutes. Thicken a little if desired. Serve with freshly boiled soft noodles. Serves about 6.

Hon. Louis A. Domotor, M.L.A.
Humboldt
Saskatchewan

Cornish Game Hens

¾ cup	soy sauce	¼ cup	melted butter
⅓ cup	Alberta honey	4	Cornish game hens
1	grated fresh ginger		salt and pepper
2	cloves garlic, mashed		

Heat together soy sauce, honey, ginger, garlic and butter. Season the hens with salt and fresh pepper, rub with a little oil and roast in a 400°F oven for 15 minutes. Remove and baste with sauce. Lower heat to 350°F, return hens to oven and continue roasting until tender, about 1 hour, basting occasionally with the sauce.

Split each hen in half and serve 1 half per person. I would suggest wild rice and a green vegetable as accompaniment.

Jack M. Campbell, M.L.A.
Rocky Mountain House
Alberta

Rolled Chicken Washington

½ cup	finely chopped fresh mushrooms OR (3 oz. can ⅔ cup) broiled chopped mushrooms, drained	dash	cayenne pepper
		1¼ cups	shredded sharp Cheddar cheese
2 tbsp.	butter OR margarine	6 or 7	boned whole chicken breasts
2 tbsp.	all-purpose flour		all-purpose flour
½ cup	light cream	2	eggs, slightly beaten
¼ tsp.	salt	¾ cup	fine dry bread crumbs

For cheese filling: Cook mushrooms in butter, about 5 minutes. Blend in flour; stir in cream. Add salt and cayenne; cook and stir until mixture becomes very thick. Stir in cheese; cook over low heat, stirring constantly, until cheese is melted. Turn mixture into pie plate. Cover; chill thoroughly, about 1 hour. Cut the firm cheese mixture into 6 or 7 equal portions; shape it into short sticks. Skin chicken breasts. To make cutlets, place each piece of chicken, boned side up, between pieces of plastic wrap. (Overlap meat where chicken breast is split.) Working out from the center, pound with wood mallet to form cutlets not quite ¼" thick. (Or ask your butcher to flatten the chicken breasts for you.) Peel off wrap. Sprinkle meat with salt. Place a cheese stick on each chicken breast. Tucking in the sides, roll chicen as for jelly roll. Press to seal well.

Dust the chicken rolls with flour; dip in slightly beaten egg, then roll in fine dry bread crumbs. Cover and chill chicken rolls thoroughly — at least 1 hour. (Or fix ahead and chill overnight.) About an hour before serving time, fry rolls in deep, hot fat 375°F, for 5 minutes or until crisp and golden brown; drain on absorbent paper towels. Place rolls in shallow baking dish and bake in slow oven, 325°F, about 30 to 45 minutes. Serve on warm platter. Makes 6 or 7 servings.

Bill Barlow, M.P.P.
Cambridge
Ontario

Wild Goose Devine à la Kim Young

"The goose should be shot from directly overhead with an 870 Remington Up using a 3" Magnum shell with a number 2 load and preferably between 11:00 a.m. and noon on a backshoot on the east side of the Saskatchewan River anywhere north of Kyle."

5-8 lb.	goose	1 cup	giblet stock
	garlic salt, to taste	½ tsp.	rosemary
	paprika, to taste	¼ tsp.	thyme
1½	stalks celery, chopped	1¼ tsp.	salt
1	carrot, chopped	1 cup	sour cream
1	onion, chopped	4 oz.	can button mushrooms,
4 tbsp.	flour		drained

Season goose inside and out with garlic salt and paprika; place on rack in shallow pan. Bake uncovered, in preheated 325°F oven for 1 hour. Sauté celery, carrot and onion in fat until soft. Blend in 2 tablespoons flour; stir in stock. Season with rosemary, thyme and salt. Stir 2 tablespoons flour into sour cream to prevent curdling during roasting. Blend sour cream into vegetables. Remove goose from pan; place in roaster. Pour sour cream and mushrooms over goose; cover. Bake 2 hours longer or until tender.

Kim Young, M.L.A.
Saskatoon Eastview
Saskatchewan

Sherried Lamb Casserole

	lamb shanks or chops	1 tsp.	thyme
2 tbsp.	butter	2	large onions, sliced
1 tsp.	salt	4-6	carrots, sliced
¼ tsp.	pepper	½ cup	dry sherry

Brown the lamb in butter over medium heat. Transfer to casserole dish or roasting pan. Sprinkle with salt, pepper and thyme. Spread the onions over the lamb, then top with carrots. Pour the sherry over this. Cover tightly and bake in a 350°F oven for 1½ hours, or until meat is tender.

A favourite of the Binns family served with baked P.E.I. potatoes and scalloped tomatoes.

Pat Binns, M.P.
Cardigan
Prince Edward Island

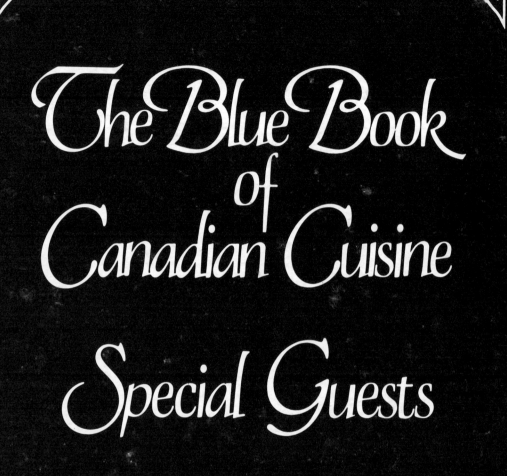

The Blue Book
of
Canadian Cuisine

Special Guests

CANADA

PRIME MINISTER · PREMIER MINISTRE

Dear Mrs. Taylor,

Mila and I are delighted to provide you with one of our favourite recipes for your Progressive Conservative cookbook. It's not often that we see the combination of good food and good politics, and we wish you every success in your endeavour.

Bon appetit!

Yours sincerely

Brian Mulroney

Veal Sour Soup

1	veal knuckle or shank	1	green pepper, seeded and coarsely chopped
10 cups	water		
	salt	2-3	cauliflower florets, coarsely chopped
½ tsp.	peppercorns		
2	fresh tomatoes, chopped	¼ cup	cup vegetable oil
1	medium potato, peeled and chopped	2 tbsp.	all-purpose flour
		½ tsp.	paprika
1	onion, sliced		juice of ½ lemon
1	stick celery, coarsely chopped	2 tbsp.	sour cream

Place veal knuckle in a large saucepan or soup kettle, add water, bring to a boil and cook, uncovered, 20 minutes. Skim off foam, then reduce heat and add salt to taste, peppercorns, tomatoes, potato and onion. Cover and simmer over low heat 1 hour.

Add celery, green pepper and cauliflower. Prepare roux by blending oil, flour and paprika in a small saucepan over medium heat. Do not brown. Add to soup and boil 10 to 15 minutes. Remove veal shank and chop meat. Strain soup into a saucepan, then pour very slowly into a tureen containing blended lemon juice and sour cream. Discard vegetables in strainer. Stir chopped veal into soup and serve.

Makes 10, 1-cup servings.

The Rt. Hon. Brian Mulroney, P.C., M.P.
The Prime Minister of Canada

Treacle Tart

8"	pre-baked shortcrust pastry flan	2 tsp.	lemon juice
	grated zest of a small lemon	6 fl. oz.	golden syrup
		2 oz.	fresh white breadcrumbs

Heat oven to 375°F.

Grate lemon zest into a bowl and place over a saucepan of hot water. Add the lemon juice and golden syrup and mix together thoroughly. Then stir in the breadcrumbs.

Using a spatula, spoon the mixture into the pastry shell.

Place the pastry on a baking tray in the centre of the oven and cook for 20 minutes or until golden brown. Serves 6.

The Rt. Hon. Margaret Thatcher, M.P.
Prime Minister of the United Kingdom of Great Britain and Northern Ireland

Rich Dark Fruit Cake

This recipe of Mme. Jehane Benoit has become a Christmas tradition in our home. A true English fruit cake, with a very good keeping quality, in Britain it is often used as wedding cake.

½ lb.	dates	2 tsp.	cinnamon
2 lbs.	seeded raisins	½ tsp.	each soda, salt and ground cloves
½ lb.	candied cherries		
½ lb.	almonds or walnuts		grated rind of 3 lemons
2 lbs.	sultana raisins	1 lb.	soft butter or margarine
1 lb.	currants	2 cups	white sugar
1 lb.	mixed peel	12	eggs
3½ cups	all-purpose flour	½ cup	cup molasses
1 tbsp.	baking powder	½ cup	grape juice or red or port wine
1 tsp.	ground coriander		
		½ cup	strong black coffee

Cut dates, seeded raisins and cherries in pieces. Blanch almonds if necessary, and slice lengthwise; chop walnuts. Place all in a large bowl with sultanas, currants and peel.

Sift flour with baking powder, spices, soda and salt. Add lemon rind. Pour 1 cupful over fruits and mix well.

Cream butter and sugar until well blended. Beat eggs until fluffy, add molasses and beat again. Add eggs to butter mixture. Beat again for 3 minutes, then add half the flour mixture and mix.

Add remaining dry ingredients and floured fruits alternately with the combined liquids. Mix thoroughly with hands and divide into prepared pans. Since this recipe yields 12 lbs. use a 10" bundt pan (5 lbs.); 9" x 4" loaf pan (3 lbs.); 10" x 5" loaf pan (4 lbs.).

Bake in a 250°F oven 3 to 3½ hours. Test with cake tester and cool completely before unmoulding.

Grant and Chantal Devine
**Hon. Grant Devine, M.L.A.
Premier of Saskatchewan**

Overnight Layered Salad

1	medium head iceburg lettuce, washed and chilled	2 tsp.	sugar
1	bunch green onions	½ cup	grated Parmesan cheese
8 oz.	can water chestnuts	1 tsp.	salt
½	red or green pepper	¼ tsp.	garlic powder
2	stalks celery	¾ lb.	bacon, crisp fried and drained
1 cup	frozen peas	3	hard-cooked eggs
2 cups	mayonnaise	2	tomatoes

Shred lettuce as you would cabbage for coleslaw. Spread over bottom of a 4-quart serving dish (glass is best). Thinly slice green onions. Scatter over lettuce. Drain water chestnuts and slice. Sprinkle over onions. Slice peppers. Sprinkle over water chestnuts. Slice celery. Sprinkle over peppers. Sprinkle frozen peas over celery. Spread mayonnaise evenly over peas. Sprinkle sugar, Parmesan cheese, salt and garlic powder on top. Coarsely chop hard-boiled eggs. Crumble bacon. Sprinkle bacon on top, then chopped eggs. Cover and chill for 4 hours or overnight. Just before serving, cut tomatoes in wedges and arrange on top of salad. Each serving should include some of each layer. 8-10 servings.

Chinese Hamburger Casserole

1 lb.	hamburger	2 tbsp.	milk
2 cups	diagonally shredded celery	2 tbsp.	soy sauce
10 oz.	pkg. thawed frozen peas	½ tsp.	pepper
¾ cup	chopped onion	1 cup	crushed potato chips
10 oz.	can condensed cream of mushroom soup		paprika

Brown hamburger without salt and place in bottom of a casserole. Put celery on top of hamburger, then a layer of thawed frozen peas. Make a sauce by mixing next 5 ingredients. Pour sauce over the peas and top with potato chips. Sprinkle paprika on top and bake at 375° for 30 minutes. Serves 6.

Grant and Chantal Devine
Hon. Grant Devine, M.L.A.
Premier of Saskatchewan

Leg of Saskatchewan Lamb

2	cloves garlic	½ cup	margarine
1	whole leg of Saskatchewan lamb	1 tbsp.	freshly squeezed lemon juice
		1 tsp.	thyme (fresh is best)

Stuff cloves of garlic into the leg at each end. Melt the margarine and mix with lemon juice and thyme, baste the leg thoroughly. Pay lots of attention to lamb while it is cooking, giving it lots of T.L.C. (Tender Loving Care). Baste it frequently and turn often so it browns evenly on all sides. Cook at 325°F using a meat thermometer until the lamb is done to your liking. We like ours on the pink side, juicy and succulent!

Sometimes I add mint jelly to the gravy until melted and then pour the hot gravy over the meat just before serving but most often serve using mint jelly on the side. Serves 4-6. This recipe has been thoroughly tested as we raise our own lamb.

Serve with creamed or baked potatoes, fresh baby carrots, broccoli.

Graham and Isabel Taylor
Hon. Graham Taylor, M.L.A.
Indian Head-Wolseley
Saskatchewan

Butterfly Leg of Lamb

4-6 lbs.	lamb	½ tsp.	oregano
2 tsp.	salt	3 tbsp.	fresh lemon juice
1 tsp.	freshly ground pepper	½ cup	Canadian dry red wine
1	clove garlic, finely minced	½ cup	salad oil
½ tsp.	thyme	1	bay leaf

Ask the butcher to bone the leg of lamb, leaving it in 1 piece, not rolled. Place meat in a large flat container of Pyrex or Corning. Sprinkle with remaining ingredients and cover with waxed paper or foil. Refrigerate 24 hours, turn meat 3-4 times in marinade. When ready to cook, remove meat from marinade, dry with paper towels.

Place meat on hot grill, immediately start to baste with marinade. Cook 6 minutes on each side. As meat cooks, continue basting meat with marinade. Meat should be well browned at this point. Lower heat and continue cooking, turning once or twice.

Medium rare takes approximately 25 minutes, depending on the fire.

John and Ann Wise
Hon. John Wise, P.C., M.P.
Elgin
Ontario

Tender Apple-Glazed Ham

4 lbs.	smoked picnic shoulder	¼ cup	liquid honey
1 cup	apple juice	2	whole garlic cloves

Preheat oven to 325°F. Place pork shoulder in a roasting pan that isn't much larger than the meat.

Stir the juice and honey together and pour over the top. Peel the garlic cloves and add them whole to the juice.

Cover tightly and bake for 20-25 minutes per pound for a shoulder that's marked "fully cooked" or 35 minutes per pound for a shoulder marked "cook before eating". Baste occasionally.

Serve with baked potatoes, squash, applesauce and crisp salad.

Hon. Charles G. Gallagher, M.L.A.
Carleton-North
New Brunswick

Ham with Curried Cranberry Glaze

My recipe is not only a favourite of my family but it is always a hit with company. In fact, this is the recipe that is most often asked for by anyone who tastes it. A bonus is that it's so simple to make and leaves me with time to do other things.

½ cup	chopped onion	16 oz.	can whole cranberry sauce
4 tsp.	curry powder	2 tbsp.	light corn syrup
4 tbsp.	butter	8-10 lb.	boneless ham

To prepare sauce: Sauté onions and curry powder in butter until onions are tender but not browned. Stir in cranberries and corn syrup. Heat through.

To bake ham: Score ham. Place on rack in a shallow pan. Bake at 350°F for 2 hours. Brush with curried cranberry sauce. Continue to bake ham another 20 minutes (check meat thermometer). Brush sauce on twice more.

Slice ham and serve, with remaining sauce served over the ham slices.

NOTE: If I use a bone-in ham I bake it with ½ cup of water and lid on for the first 2 hours.

Hon. Joan H. Duncan, M.L.A.
Maple Creek
Saskatchewan

Grilled Ham Slice

½ cup	grape jelly OR more tart jelly, if preferred	1½ tsp.	lemon juice
2 tbsp.	prepared mustard	⅛ tsp.	ground cinnamon
		1½ lb.	fully cooked centre-cut ham slice, 1" thick

In a saucepan, combine jelly, mustard, lemon juice, and cinnamon. Heat until jelly melts. Slash fat edge of ham slice. Pour sauce over ham in a shallow dish. Refrigerate overnight or let stand at room temperature for 2 hours, spooning sauce over ham several times. Remove ham, reserving marinade.

Broil ham over low coals 5 minutes on each side. Brush one side of ham with marinade; turn. Broil brushed side 3 minutes. Repeat with other side, broiling 3 minutes longer. Heat remaining marinade on edge of grill. Serve with ham. Makes 6 servings.

Pork chops may be substituted for the ham slice.

Peter Elzinga, M.P.
Pembina
Alberta

Garlic Pork and Onions

1 lb.	pork tenderloin	3 tbsp.	white wine
3-4 tbsp.	cornstarch	2	medium onions, sliced
2-3	garlic cloves, minced		salt and pepper, to taste
5 tbsp.	soy sauce		

If possible use a wok for cooking. Cut pork into small pieces, coat meat with mixture of cornstarch and garlic, add soy sauce. Let stand for at least ½ an hour or more. Fry in hot oil, separating pieces of meat; cook until meat loses its colour, add wine and stir, push meat to one side, add onion slices and sauté. Salt and pepper if desired.
NOTE: A can of cream of mushroom soup can be added if a gravy is wanted. Serve with noodles; lightly fried bean sprouts are also great.

Hon. Reuben Baetz, M.P.P.
Ottawa West
Ontario

Pork Tenderloin with Rosemary-Apple Sauce

1 tbsp.	butter	2 cups	frozen carrots OR 14 oz. can carrots, drained
1	pork tenderloin, about ¾ lb.		
¾ cup	apple juice	½ cup	sour cream
½ tsp.	rosemary, crumbled salt, pepper and garlic to taste		

Melt butter in a large frying pan. Slice tenderloin into ⅓" rounds. Sauté in butter until lightly browned on both sides. Add apple juice to pan. Sprinkle with seasonings and bring to a boil. If using frozen carrots, add to pan. Cover, reduce heat and simmer for 10 minutes, stirring occasionally. If using canned carrots add to pan during last few minutes of cooking just to heat through. Using a slotted spatula, remove the meat and carrots from pan. Keep warm.

Boil sauce vigorously until it reduces to about ¼ cup and just covers the bottom of the pan, about 5 minutes. Stir in sour cream. Pour over meat and carrots. Serves 3.

Hon. R. H. Ramsay, M.P.P.
Sault Ste. Marie
Ontario

Pork Tenderloin with Pepper

¼ tbsp.	crushed black peppercorns	½ cup	whipping cream
¾ lb.	pork tenderloin	1 tbsp.	Dijon mustard
3 tbsp.	butter	pinch	each thyme, marjoram and rosemary
3 tbsp.	brandy		

Cut tenderloin into pieces and pound to ¼" thickness. Pound pepper into cutlets. Fry in butter until browned.

Mix brandy, cream, mustard and spices. Pour over meat. Cover and bake for 20 minutes.

Hon. Tom Siddon, P.C., M.P.
Richmond-South Delta
British Columbia

Pork Tenderloin Voyageur

6	small pork tenderloins, trimmed	1 tbsp.	flour
		2 cups	whipping cream
	salt, white pepper, thyme, aromat to taste	1	apple, peeled and diced
		½ cup	raisins
½ cup	flour	½ cup	pitted dried prunes, quartered
¾ cup	butter		
1	lemon	1 tbsp.	chopped parsley
¼ cup	dry white wine		

Cut pork in 2 oz. pieces. Flatten out to approximately ¼" thickness. Season with salt, pepper, thyme, aromat. Dust with flour. Brown meat in ½ cup butter. Remove and keep warm. Deglaze frying pan with juices from lemon and the wine. Simmer until reduced to half the volume. Blend in 1 tbsp. flour to make a light roux. Slowly add cream and simmer 5 minutes. In separate frying pan sauté apples, raisins and prunes in remaining butter until apples are transparent. Arrange meat on platter, cover with sauce, garnish with sautéed fruits and parsley. Garnish with julienned lemon peel. Serves 6.

William C. Attewell, M.P.
Don Valley East
Ontario

Pork Schnitzel

4	slices boneless leg of pork, ¼" thick	½ tsp.	salt
		⅛ tsp.	pepper or lemon pepper
½ cup	flour	½ cup	butter
1	egg, slightly beaten	1	lemon, cut in wedges
1 tbsp.	water	2	eggs, hard-cooked
1½ cups	dry bread crumbs		

Pound pork slices thin. Dredge thoroughly with flour. Dip floured meat in egg and water mixture. Shake meat in bag with spiced crumbs. Refrigerate meat 1 hour to dry. Heat butter on griddle. Fry meat to golden brown, 4 minutes each side. Serve immediately, garnished with lemon and egg wedges. DELICIOUS!!

Sid and Vel Fraleigh
Sid Fraleigh, M.P.
Lambton - Middlesex
Ontario

Sweet and Sour Spareribs

1 cup	brown sugar	1 tsp.	paprika
1 tbsp.	salt	12 oz.	can tomato juice
1 tbsp.	celery seed	½ cup	vinegar
1 tbsp.	chili powder	1	rack of ribs, about 2 lbs.

Combine sugar, salt, celery seed, chili powder and paprika in bowl.

Place ribs in roasting pan and rub with half of above mixture, place under broiler until ribs are very brown. Turn ribs and rub with remaining half of mixture, place under broiler until very brown.

Combine tomato juice and vinegar and pour over ribs. Bake covered at 425°F to 450°F for 1 hour, basting frequently, or turn ribs once during baking.

Jack Johnson, M.P.P.
Wellington-Dufferin-Peel
Ontario

Sweet and Sour Spareribs

2 lbs.	spareribs	2 tbsp.	soy sauce
¼ cup	sugar	3 tbsp.	vinegar
½ tsp.	dry mustard	1 cup	water
½ tsp.	salt	1 cup	ketchup
2 tbsp.	flour		

Cut ribs into small pieces and brown in oil. Mix remaining ingredients in order given and pour over spareribs. Cook at 350°F for 1 hour.

Hon. Neal Hardy, M.L.A.
Kelsey-Tisdale
Saskatchewan

Spareribs

2 lbs.	pork ribs, cut apart		
Sauce:			
19 oz.	can stewed tomatoes	1 tsp.	salt
10 oz.	can tomato soup	2 tbsp.	Worcestershire sauce
1 tsp.	dry mustard		little lemon juice
1 tbsp.	brown sugar	drop	Tabasco sauce

Place ribs on broiler pan and broil until all fat is crisp and dry. (This takes quite awhile.) Mix all sauce ingredients in a small roaster. Add drained ribs. Mix. Cover and bake at 350°F 1½-2 hours.

Serves 4-6. Serve with rice and stir-fry vegetables.

Carl and Vania Paproski
Carl Paproski, M.L.A.
Edmonton Kingsway
Alberta

Pork Rib Dinner

4 lbs.	pork loin chops	2 lbs.	small red potatoes
⅓ cup	all-purpose flour	16 oz.	pkg. of carrots, cut in 2"
2 tbsp.	salad oil		pieces
1½ cups	apple juice	1 lb.	whole small onions
1 tbsp.	salt	1	small head cabbage, shredded
½ tsp.	pepper		

About 2½ hours before serving, on waxed paper, coat chops with flour. Reserve leftover flour. In 8-quart Dutch oven, over medium-high heat, in hot salad oil, cook meat, a few pieces at a time, until well browned on both sides. Remove pieces as they brown. Reduce heat to medium. Into drippings in Dutch oven, stir reserved flour until blended. Gradually stir in apple juice. Return meat to Dutch oven; add salt and pepper; heat to boiling. Cover Dutch oven and bake in 350°F oven 30 minutes. Add potatoes, carrots and onions; cover; bake 30 minutes. Skim off fat from liquid in Dutch oven. Add cabbage; cover and bake 1 hour longer or until vegetables and meat are tender, stirring occasionally. Makes 8 servings.

Lloyd and Cheryl Sauter
Lloyd Sauter, M.L.A.
Nipawin
Saskatchewan

Tourtière Du Lac St. Jean

This recipe originated with my mother, Mrs. Emilie Bédard Côté.

Dough:

5 cups	flour	2 tsp.	baking powder
1 lb.	Crisco shortening	1 tsp.	salt
	water		

Filling:

2 lbs.	pork		salt pork, optional or to taste
1 lb.	beef		potatoes, cubed (same
1	chicken		amount as meat)
	onions		water
	salt and pepper		

Mix dry ingredients, cut in shortening and add enough water, about 2 glasses, so dough will be easy to handle. Put in refrigerator for a few hours. Cut pork, beef and chicken into 1" cubes. If you are lucky enough to have some, you can also add wild meat: deer, moose, partridge or rabbit. Add onion, salt, pepper and salt pork. Leave overnight in refrigerator. Roll out dough to cover bottom and sides of roasting pan. Add the meat and potatoes and enough water to cover all. Roll out a piece of dough to cover all. Make a few steam vents on top of crust. (When my children were young, I used to roll long strips of dough and then twist them and add on top of crust, that way each child had his own little "bird".)

Cook at 400°F for about 1 hour, until meat starts to boil, then lower oven to 275°F-300°F and cook another 3½ to 4 hours, until top crust is golden brown.

Clément Côté, M.P.
Lac Saint-Jean
Quebec

Tourtière

A traditional French-Canadian dish for Christmas

Pastry:

⅔ cup	shortening	1 tsp.	salt
3 tbsp.	butter	4 tbsp.	cold water
2 cups	stirred but unsifted all-purpose flour		

Filling:

2 lbs.	ground fresh pork (I prefer butt of the leg, but shoulder can be used. Not sausage meat.)	1	medium-large carrot, ground
		2	medium-small potatoes, ground
		1½ tsp.	salt
1	small onion OR ⅛ Spanish onion, ground	⅛ tsp.	pepper
		½ cup	hot water

Make pastry by cutting shortening and butter into flour and salt until size of peas. Drizzle in water, 1 tablespoon at a time, tossing with fork until flour is dampened, then press into a ball. Divide and roll out half of dough to fit 9" x 1¼" pie plate. Roll out other half, gash to allow steam to escape. Let rest on board while you make FILLING: In large frying pan over high heat sear ground pork until fat renders out, chopping and stirring all the while to break up chunks. Discard excess fat, but leave enough to keep the meat moist and tender.

Put onion through grinder first, add to meat in pan and sauté until onion is limp but not brown. Remove from heat. Put carrot and potatoes through grinder (approximately 1¼ cups of ground potatoes and carrot.) Add to meat mixture along with salt, pepper and water. Mix well. Turn into pastry-lined pie plate.

NOTE: This is a lot of meat filling, but pile it in and smooth top. Seal on gashed top crust and crimp edges snugly. Glaze top liberally by brushing with 1 egg yolk mixed with 1 tablespoon water. Bake at 450°F for 10 minutes, then reduce heat to 325°F for 30 minutes then reduce again to 300°F for 20 minutes.

Paul and Janine Rousseau
Hon. Paul Rousseau, M.L.A.
Regina South
Saskatchewan

Tourtière

This French meat pie is traditionally served on Christmas Eve. It may be warmed up to serve the latecomers, if there is any left.

5 lbs.	ground pork		2	onions
1½ cups	boiling water			salt and pepper
1	clove garlic			cloves, nutmeg, cinnamon
2	potatoes, grated			

Boil meat in water for about 1 hour, adding garlic, potatoes, onions, salt and pepper, a little cloves, nutmeg and cinnamon, until meat is whitish in color.

Cool and put in uncooked, pastry-lined pie plates and bake in medium oven 350°F until crust is brown, about 50-60 minutes.

Jim and Angel Garner
Hon. J. W. A. Garner, M.L.A.
Wilkie
Saskatchewan

Jellied Pork Hocks (Head Cheese or Sültz)

4-6	pork hocks	1 tsp.	salt
	water	¼ tsp.	pepper
⅓ cup	chopped onion		dill weed
2	carrots, sliced		parsley
3	stalks celery, sliced	1	pkg. gelatin

Put pork hocks in a large pot, fill ¾ full with water. For added flavor add some or all of the vegetables and seasonings. Simmer for 3-4 hours. When the meat is cooked remove from the pot and cut up the meat (and skin, optional), put in a bowl or bread pan. For extra firmness you may add gelatin to the juice and bring to a boil, then strain the juice into the bowl with meat. Add enough juice to cover the meat well. Cook, then put in refrigerator to gel.

Arnold Tusa, M.L.A.
Last Mountain-Touchwood
Saskatchewan

Cervelles Au Beurre Noir

3	pairs calves' brains		seasoned flour
	water		clarified butter
	vinegar		cognac

Soak calves' brains in cold water, add a little white vinegar and cover for 1 hour. Remove the membrane and any traces of blood. Rinse the brains in ice-cold water, drain them. Dry them with a towel and cut them in 3 or 4 pieces each. Drop each piece into seasoned flour. Sauté them in a skillet in clarified butter until they are nicely browned and crispy. Flambé with cognac and serve.

L'hon. Robert de Cotret, P.C., M.P.
Berthier-Maskinongé-Lanaudiére
Québec

Braised Veal Loin

6-7 lb.	boned loin of veal	4	shallots, chopped
1 or 2	veal kidneys	1	bouquet garni
	salt, pepper	2	carrots, sliced
	fines herbes	1 cup	white wine
	butter	20	very small onions
3	onions, finely chopped	1 lb.	small mushrooms

Stuff the loin with the kidneys. Season well inside and out with salt, pepper and fines herbes.

Brown the meat in butter and add the chopped onions, shallots, bouquet garni, and carrots. Season with salt and pepper. Add wine, cover and simmer 30 minutes per pound. Turn once or twice during cooking.

Place the 20 small onions with 1 tablespoon of butter and enough water to half cover them in another pot. Add a pinch of salt and sugar and cook slowly until all the water has evaporated. Cook mushrooms in the same way.

Serve the roast surrounded by the mushrooms and onions glazed with some of the juices from the roast. Serve the rest of the juices separately. Serves 8.

Hon. John Bosley, M.P.
Speaker of the house,
Don Valley West
Ontario

Beef Tenderloin

This recipe makes a lovely meal with very little effort.

1	tenderloin of beef	salad oil
1	garlic clove	

Remove surface fat and connective tissue from meat and rub surface with garlic. Place tenderloin on a rack in shallow pan, tucking narrow end of meat under to make roast uniformly thick. Brush with salad oil and insert a roast meat thermometer. Roast in a 450°F oven until meat thermometer reads 140°F (rare), about 45 to 60 minutes for a 4 to 6 pound whole tenderloin or 45 to 50 minutes for a half tenderloin.

Bob and Lynne Andrew
Hon. R. L. Andrew, M.L. A.
Kindersley
Saskatchewan

Scallopini Alla Mozzarella

¼ tasse	de farine	1		boîte (14 oz.) de sauce á spaghetti Gattuso
¼ c. à thé	de poivre			
4	escalopes de veau ou de poulet, chacune d'environ ¼ po. d'épaisseur	1		grosse gousse d'ail émincée
		1 c. à thé		de feuilles d'origan broyées
2 c. à	soupe de beurre non salé	4		tranches de fromage suisse

Mélanger farine et poivre sur du papier ciré. Fariner les escalopes. Dans une poêle de 10 pouces, à feu modéré, dans le beurre chaud, faire cuire les escalopes 3 ou 4 minutes de chaque côté jusqu'à ce qu'elles soient dorées. Mettre sur une assiette. Dans la même poêle, verser la sauce à spaghetti, ail et origan. Amener à ébullition et baisser le feu. Remettre les escalopes dans la casserole et garnir de fromage suisse. Cuire jusqu'á ce que le fromage commence à fondre. Pour 4 personnes.
Bon appétit!

L'hon Roch LaSalle, P.C. M.P.
Joliette
Québec

Mike's Marinated Barbecued Steak

5-6 lb.   sirloin steak, 2¼" thick, in 1
              piece

Marinade:

½ cup	olive oil	1	small onion
¼ cup	lemon juice	1 or 2	cloves garlic
½	carrot	½ tsp.	salt
½	stalk celery	6	sprigs parsley

Trim all fat from meat, debone. Put marinade ingredients in blender or food processor and mix until puréed. Marinate steak in refrigerator for minimum of 3 hours (best overnight). This marinade may also be used for shish kabobs.

Place skewers in meat to hold together and help turn meat on barbecue rack. Cook on hot open barbecue — do not close lid on barbecue. Cooking approximately 20 minutes each side for medium-rare. Cut steak into slices on bias. Serves 6-8 people.

Michael Harris, M.P.P.
Nipissing
Ontario

Savoury Pepper Steak

1½ lb.	beef round steak	½ cup	chopped onion
½ tsp.	salt	1	small clove garlic, minced
⅛ tsp.	pepper	1 tbsp.	beef gravy base
¼ cup	shortening	½ tsp.	Worcestershire sauce
19 oz.	can tomatoes	1	large green pepper
1¾ cups	water		

Cut beef in ½" thick strips, sprinkle with salt and pepper. In large skillet, brown strips in hot shortening. Drain tomatoes, reserving liquid. Add reserved liquid, water, onion, garlic, gravy base to meat. Cover, simmer 1¼ hours or until meat is tender. Uncover, stir in Worcestershire sauce. Cut green pepper in strips, add to meat. Cover; simmer meat and peppers for 5 minutes. If gravy is too thin, combine 1-2 tbsp. all-purpose flour with an equal amount of cold water, stir into sauce. Cook and stir until thickened and bubbly. Add chopped tomatoes, cook 5 minutes or more. Serve over hot cooked rice.

Gordon Taylor, M.P.
Bow River
Alberta

Cold Fillet of Beef and Veal with Mustard Sauce

3½ lb.	(net weight) fillet of beef, completely trimmed	½ tsp.	white pepper
3 lb.	(net weight) eye of loin of veal, completely trimmed	½ cup	coarsely chopped celery
		½ cup	coarsely chopped onion
		½ cup	coarsely chopped carrot
	olive oil	2	cloves garlic, crushed
1 tsp.	salt		

Preheat oven to 450°F. Place beef fillet next to veal, cut off ends of the beef so that fillet is the same length as the loin of veal. Quickly sear beef on all sides and both ends in frying pan in a little oil, about 1 minute. Set beef aside to cool. Split loin of veal lengthwise without cutting it all the way through (butterfly cut). Open veal out flat, and season inside with salt and pepper. Lay beef down the centre of veal and wrap the veal around it to enclose it completely. (If veal is not wide enough to wrap beef entirely, open it up, and pound with the flat side of a cleaver to flatten it.) Tie the meat at intervals with kitchen string. Place meat in a lightly oiled roasting pan, roast it for 15 minutes. Remove pan from oven and reduce temperature to 370°F. Remove meat from pan and scatter celery, onion, carrot and garlic in bottom of the pan. Place meat on top of vegetables and roast for an additional 25 minutes. Set meat and vegetables to cool.

Mustard Sauce:

1 cup	dry white wine	2	shallots, finely chopped
1	bay leaf	½ cup	Dijon-style mustard
½ tsp.	crushed black peppercorns	½ cup	heavy cream
¼ tsp.	thyme	½ cup	chopped chives
½ cup	tarragon vinegar		

To prepare the mustard sauce, deglaze the pan with white wine and scrape the mixture into a small saucepan. Add the bay leaf, peppercorns, thyme, vinegar and shallots; reduce over high heat until about ¼ cup of liquid remains. Strain and set aside to cool. In a mixing bowl, whisk the mustard with a heavy cream. Stir in the cooled reduction. Just before serving, stir in the chives. When ready to serve, slice the meat into ½" slices and serve with the cooled vegetables. Serve the mustard sauce on the side.
Serves 10.

Hon. Bud Gregory, M.P.P.
Mississauga East
Ontario

Quick and Easy Pepper Steak

1 lb.	round steak	1	medium onion, coarsely chopped
2 tbsp.	vegetable oil		
	salt and pepper	1	green pepper, chopped
	garlic powder OR salt to taste	1 cup	fresh OR canned mushrooms
		1	tomato, chopped (optional)
	soy sauce		

In a large skillet or wok, brown cubed round steak in vegetable oil. Season with salt, pepper, garlic powder and soy sauce to suit your taste. When meat is nearly cooked, turn down heat and add, onion, pepper, mushrooms and simmer for 10 minutes. Add tomato and let simmer for another 5 minutes.

Serve with cooked rice.

Hon. Paul J. Schoenhals, M.L.A.
Saskatoon Sutherland
Saskatchewan

Rouladen

4	rouladen	1	small onion
	mustard	2	slices bacon
	salt and pepper	10 oz.	can bouillon
1	pickle		

If prepared rouladen is not available, pound serving-size pieces of round steak ⅛"-¼" thick. Unroll 1 rouladen. Spread with mustard, sprinkle with salt and pepper. Quarter pickle and onion lengthwise. At 1 end place ¼ of the pickle, ¼ of the onion and ¼ of the bacon. Roll up the rouladen. Secure with a toothpick. Repeat with other 3. Brown on all sides and then add the bouillon. Put in oven 350°F for 2 hours.

James R. McPherson, M.L.A.
Red Deer
Alberta

Fondue Bourgignonne

La recette de la sauce m'a été donnée par des amis avocats en Suisse. Pour 6 personnes.

1 litre	d'huile d'arachide	2 kilos	de cubes de boeuf (soit filet mignon ou coeur de pointe de surlonge) sans gras

Recette de la sauce:

1 tasse ½	d'eau chaude	1 cuil.	soupe de curry
½ tasse	de vinaigre blanc	2 ou 3	gouttes de tabasco
⅔ tasse	d'huile d'olive ou crisco	1 boîte	d'anchois ou tube de purée d'anchois
1 cuil.	soupe comble de farine		
1 cuil.	soupe de moutarde de Dijon	1 petit	pot de câpres égouttées
	soupe de purée de tomate	2 paquets	d'échalottes coupées finement
1 cuil.	soupe comble de paprika	1 paquet	de persil coupé finement
1 cuil.			

Amener à ébulition et bouillir ensemble 10 minutes à feu moyen l'eau et le vinaigre. Ajouter le ⅔ de tasse d'huile dans laquelle on a délayé la farine et bouillir à feu vif durant une minute pour l'obtention d'une suace blanche épaisse (si trop épaisse et que l'huile ressort ajouter un peu d'eau). Laisser refroidir.

Ajouter à la base de sauce, la moutarde de Dijon, la purée de tomate, le paprika, le curry, le tabasco. Si vous n'avez pas trouvé de purée d'anchoi, prendre une partie de la sauce, la placer dans un Blender et ajouter une boîte de filet d'anchois avec l'huile. Actionner pour rendre en purée et ajouter à la sauce. Bien brasser.

Finir la sauce en ajoutant les câpres, le persil, et les échalottes coupées finement. Bien mélanger. Peut être fait de 3 à 6 heures avant ou immédiatement avant.

Chauffer l'huile d'archide dans le cagnelon sur le poêle jusqu'à ce que l'on ajoute une fourchette sur laquelle est piqué un cube de viande et que le morceau cuit immédiatement. Amener sur la table le cagnelon que l'on dépose sur le réchaud et chacun cuit sa viande á son goût.

Contrairement à la France, en Suisse on ne sert que cette sauce avec les cubes de viande. Ce met se mange avec une salade verte et vinaigrette huile et vinaigre accompagné de pain français croustillant et pomme de terre au four. Je le sers sans pomme de terre et avec un vin de bourgogne ou un beaujolais.

Suzanne Duplessis, M.P.
Louis-Hébert
Québec

Beef Stroganoff

This is my wife Catherine's recipe. It is my favourite and I can certainly vouch for its outstanding success in my own large family.

3 lb.	sirloin roast	½	soup can water
1 cup	chopped onion		garlic salt
1 cup	sliced mushrooms		sour cream
2 x 10 oz.	cans cream of mushroom soup		

Cut meat into bite-sized strips. Brown in hot fat, then cook in pressure cooker until tender. Sauté and add onion and mushrooms. Heat together soup, water and garlic salt, and pour over meat. Add sour cream just before serving.

Neil and Catherine Crawford
Hon. Neil Crawford, M.L.A.
Edmonton Parkallen
Alberta

Shrake's Beef Strogonoff

1 lb.	round steak	¼ tsp.	Tabasco sauce
⅓ cup	butter	1 cup	water OR consommé
1	clove garlic	6 oz.	tin mushrooms
½ cup	chopped onion	½ cup	wine
1 tsp.	salt	1 cup	sour cream
½ tsp.	pepper		

Cut steak in small cubes. Melt butter in frying pan; crush garlic; add it with onions. Cook until clear; add beef and spices. Brown well. Remove garlic. Add mushrooms, water and wine, simmer until done. Add wine. Do not boil. Just before serving add sour cream. Serve with noodles or rice. Serves 4.

Gordon Shrake, M.L.A.
Calgary Millican
Alberta

Easy Beef Stroganoff

1	large sirloin steak	1	envelope dry onion soup mix
10 oz.	can sliced mushrooms, including liquid	2 tbsp.	flour
		1 cup	sour cream
⅔ cup	water		

Slice steak in thin strips cutting with the grain of the meat. Brown meat in small amount of oil in a frying pan. Add sliced mushrooms and liquid and water. When mixture bubbles, add dry soup mix. Add flour to sour cream and mix thoroughly. Bring mixture to a boil and add sour cream mixture, stirring until blended. Serve over rice or noodles.

Elliott Hardey, M.P.
Kent
Ontario

Baxter's Beef Burgundy

1½ lbs.	beef top round	4	slices bacon
8 oz.	bottle Catalina salad dressing	¼ tsp.	pepper
10 oz.	can cream of mushroom soup	2 cups	burgundy wine
		12	small white whole onions
14 oz.	can jellied cranberry sauce	8 oz.	can stewed tomatoes
dash	soy sauce	1 cup	sliced mushrooms
dash	Worcestershire sauce		

Cut beef into 1¼" cubes. Marinate meat all night in salad dressing, soup, cranberry, soy and Worcestershire sauces. In large saucepan cook bacon until crisp, remove and crumble and set aside. In same saucepan, add marinated meat with sauces, add pepper and wine. Cover and cook over low heat for 1½ hours. Add onions, tomatoes and mushrooms. Cover and cook for approximately 2 hours more, over low heat, or until meat is tender. Serve over wide noodles. Garnish with bacon and parsley. Serves 8.

Hon. John B. M. Baxter, Q.C., M.L.A.
Kings West
New Brunswick

Alphabet Pot Roast

3-4 lb.	beef pot roast	½ cup	red dry wine
	salt and pepper	⅛ tsp.	dried basil
10 oz.	can alphabet OR vegetable soup	2 tbsp.	finely chopped parsley

Sprinkle beef with salt and pepper. Place in a slow cooker pot. In a small mixing bowl combine undiluted soup with the wine and basil. Pour over the meat. Cover and cook on low for 8 to 10 hours. Sprinkle with parsley. Slice meat, serve sauce ladled over the meat. (Sauce may be thickened with flour dissolved in a small amount of water.) Makes 6 to 8 servings.

Alan W. Hyland, M.L.A.
Cypress
Alberta

Meadow Lake Stampede Stew

1½-2 lbs.	stewing beef OR round steak	1 tbsp.	Worcestershire sauce
	flour, salt and pepper	1 tbsp.	steak sauce
¼ cup	oil	½ tsp.	thyme
6	medium onions, thinly sliced	2-3	bay leaves
1 tsp.	garlic salt OR powder	2-3 cups	tomato juice
1	bottle beer	3	potatoes, diced
1 tsp.	soy sauce	3	carrots
		½ pkg.	frozen green peas

Cube meat. Mix flour, salt and pepper. Coat meat with flour mixture. Heat oil in large frying pan. Brown the meat, add onion and garlic, cook until onion is transparent. Add beer, soy sauce, Worcestershire, steak sauce, thyme and bay leaves. Bring to a boil, cover, reduce heat and simmer for an hour. Add tomato juice, simmer 30 minutes. Add potatoes and carrots, cook for 20 minutes. Add peas 10 minutes before serving. Remove bay leaves. Can be stretched easily for unexpected company. Serves 6.

George, Karen, Natasha and Trevor McLeod
Hon. George McLeod, M.L.A.
Meadow Lake
Saskatchewan

Barbados Beef Stew

"I never found this when I visited Barbados, but my Mother got this recipe 25 years ago from a friend who went to Barbados."

3 lb.	shoulder OR stewing beef in ½" cubes	⅓ cup	cider vinegar
		⅓ cup	molasses
3 tbsp.	flour	1 cup	water
1 tbsp.	fat	6	carrots, chunked
1½ cups	canned tomatoes	½ cup	raisins
2	medium onions, sliced	1 tsp.	salt
½ tsp.	ginger	¼ tsp.	pepper
1 tsp.	celery salt		

Sprinkle beef with flour. Brown in fat and add tomatoes, onions, ginger and celery salt. Combine vinegar, molasses and water and add to meat. Cover and simmer 1½ hour. Add carrots. Simmer 45 minutes. Add raisins, salt and pepper. Simmer 15 minutes. Serve with mashed potatoes, parsley garnish and a green vegetable.

Paul and Sandra McCrossan
W. Paul McCrossan, M.P.
York-Scarborough
Ontario

Bacon-Wrapped Hamburgers

1½ lbs.	hamburger	½	small green pepper, chopped
1	egg	¼ cup	lemon juice
½ cup	water	1 tsp.	salt
¼ cup	dry bread crumbs	½ tsp.	instant beef bouillon
1	small onion, chopped	6-7	thin slices bacon, halved

Mix all ingredients except bacon. Shape mixture into 6 or 7 patties, each about ¾" thick. Criss-cross 2 half slices bacon on each patty, tucking ends under. Place patties on rack in shallow roasting pan. Cook uncovered in 350°F oven 50 minutes. 6 or 7 servings.

Lloyd E. Hampton, M.L.A.
Canora
Saskatchewan

Pat's Pot-Pourri

2	eggs	2 tbsp.	horseradish
2 lbs.	ground beef (chuck is preferable)	¼ cup	milk
		¼ cup	ketchup
2 cups	soft bread crumbs	1 tsp.	dry mustard
¾ cup	minced onion	½ cup	ketchup (optional)
¼ cup	diced green pepper		

Break eggs into large bowl and beat lightly with a fork. Add ground meat, and toss lightly until blended. Add the bread crumbs, minced onion, and diced pepper. Mix the horseradish with the next three ingredients. Add horseradish mixture to the meat mixture and combine lightly; too much mixing tends to toughen the meat loaf. Shape into a loaf, and place in lightly greased loaf pan. Spread with ½ cup of ketchup if desired. Bake in moderate oven, 350°F, about 1½ to 2 hours. Allow to sit in pan for 10 minutes before turning out to slice. Delicious hot or served cold.

Pat Nowlan, M.P.
Annapolis Valley-Hants
Nova Scotia

Quick and Easy Meat Loaf

⅔ cup	bread crumbs	½ cup	grated onions
1 cup	milk	1 tsp.	salt
1½ lbs.	minced beef	¼ tsp.	pepper
2	eggs, well-beaten	½ tsp.	sage OR marjoram
Devilled Sauce:			
3 tbsp.	brown sugar	¼ tsp.	nutmeg
¼ cup	ketchup	1 tsp.	dry mustard

Soak the bread crumbs in milk for 20 minutes. Add the remaining meat loaf ingredients. Blend well. Turn into a buttered loaf pan. Cover with the spiced sauce. Cook in a 350°F oven, 1 hour.

Noble A. Villeneuve, M.P.P.
Stormont-Dundas-Glengarry
Ontario

Meat Loaf

¼ cup	ketchup	1¼ tsp.	salt
2 tbsp.	lemon juice	⅛ tsp.	pepper
1 tbsp.	brown sugar	1	egg
½ tsp.	dry mustard	½ cup	dry bread crumbs
1	onion	1 lb.	minced steak
2 tbsp.	water		

Mix first 10 ingredients together and add to steak. Place in prepared loaf pan. Bake about 1 hour at 350°F.

William and Elizabeth Winegard
William C. Winegard, M.P.
Guelph
Ontario

Lasagna

This is a favorite of mine. I am a direct descendant of United Empire Loyalists of German background who came from Bucks Co., Pennsylvania and I prefer Italian Food.

1	medium onion	1	tomato paste can water
2	cloves garlic	6	lasagne noodles, cooked
1 lb.	hamburger	1 cup	cottage cheese
2 tbsp.	oil	1	egg
2 tbsp.	parsley	8 oz.	mozzarella cheese, grated
3 tbsp.	oregano	¼ cup	grated Parmesan cheese
19 oz.	can tomatoes		mozzarella slices
5 oz.	can tomato paste		

Sauté onion, garlic and hamburger in oil until light brown. Add next 5 ingredients and simmer ¾ hour. Cook lasagne noodles. Beat egg into cottage cheese. In 9" x 13" pan layer: ½ of sauce, 3 noodles, the grated mozzarella, ½ the cottage cheese mixture, 2 tbsp. Parmesan, remainder of sauce, 3 noodles, remainder of cottage cheese mixture, other 2 tbsp. Parmesan. Top with sliced mozzarella. Bake at 350°F for 30 minutes.

Hazen E. Myers, M.L.A.
Kings East
New Brunswick

Andy Brandt's Favourite Spaghetti Recipe

Sauce:

2 x 28 oz.	cans tomatoes		¾ tsp.	crushed chili
5 oz.	can tomato paste		¾ tsp.	tarragon
3	bay leaves		1 tsp.	ground parsley
¼	green pepper		¾ tsp.	oregano
¼	sweet red pepper		1 tsp.	sweet basil
1	celery stalk		1 tsp.	celery salt
3	garlic cloves		½ tsp.	curry powder
1	small onion		1½ tsp.	chili powder
4 tbsp.	vegetable oil			

Mix tomatoes and tomato paste with 3 bay leaves. Let simmer for 1 hour. While simmering sauce, finely chop green peppers, red peppers, celery, garlic cloves and onion, and sauté in vegetable oil until soft. Add to tomato sauce.

Reserve oil to cook meatballs. Also add to tomato sauce: crushed chilies, tarragon, parsley, oregano, basil, celery salt, curry powder and chili powder.

Meatballs:

1½ lbs.	beef, pork and veal, ground and mixed		1 tsp.	parsley
			½ tsp.	curry powder
¼ cup	bread crumbs		1 tsp.	celery salt
1	egg, beaten		½ tsp.	poultry seasoning
1 tsp.	basil		1 tsp.	chili powder
1 tsp.	garlic powder		½ tsp.	crushed chilies

Combine meatball ingredients thoroughly. Shape into small balls, roll in bread crumbs. Fry in oil until browned, drain. Add to sauce, simmer for 3 hours.

Hon. Andrew S. Brandt, M.P.P.
Sarnia
Ontario

Kroeger's Steak and Vegetables

Easy to do in any quantity, this dish is great for a man having to do the dinner on his own. I use this recipe for a fast family dinner, for any size group.

steak	sliced onions
sliced potatoes	sliced celery
sliced carrots	

Cut steak into small cubes and brown in a fairly hot pan. Bring sliced vegetables to boil in a fairly large pot. When beef is dark brown, add to the boiling vegetables, including all the juices from the steak.

This can be converted into stew in minutes if you prefer.

Henry Kroeger, M.L.A.
Chinook
Alberta

"Yum-Yum"

Hope you enjoy this favorite which I swiped from my wife's well-used culinary list.

1 lb.	hamburger	1 cup	raw rice
1	large onion, chopped	1 cup	chopped celery
10 oz.	can cream of mushroom soup	2 cups	water
		4 tbsp.	soy sauce
10 oz.	can cream of chicken soup		Chinese noodles

Brown hamburger, add onion and sauté until softened. Mix in the soups and a little water used to rinse soup cans. Combine this with rice, celery, water and soy sauce.

Turn into buttered casserole and bake for 1 hour.

For the last 20 minutes add a generous topping of Chinese noodles.

Hon. Cyril B. Sherwood,
The Senate
New Brunswick

Klondike Goulash

2 lbs.	ground steak (not too fat)	10 oz.	can ripe olives, black, pitted, chopped in circles
1 tsp.	salt	1	pkg. noodles (⅛-¼" width)
	pepper	¼ lb.	old Cheddar cheese, grated
2	onions, finely chopped	1 cup	cracker crumbs, put in plastic bag and crushed
2	green peppers, chopped		
2 x 12 oz.	cans niblet corn	1	clove of garlic, chopped OR dash of garlic powder
14 oz.	can tomatoes		
6 oz.	can tomato paste	10 oz.	can mushroom soup
10 oz.	can mushrooms		

Brown meat with salt and some pepper. Add onions, peppers, corn, tomatoes, tomato paste, mushrooms, olives and cook for 10 minutes stirring frequently. Cook 1 pkg. fine noodles in salted boiling water, then drain. Put noodles in a flat dish (about 3" or 4" deep). Pour meat mixture over them. Heat mushroom soup, pour over meat mixture. Sprinkle crumbs and cheese mixture over all. Dot with dabs of butter and cover with lid or tin foil. Bake in a moderate oven, 350°F for 50 minutes. Remove lid and bake for 10 minutes or more allowing it to brown.

Bea Firth, M.L.A.
Whitehorse Riverdale South
Yukon

Wild Rice Casserole

1 cup	uncooked wild rice	1	soup can water
1 lb.	hamburger	½ cup	each diced celery and onion
10 oz.	can mushrooms, drained	1 tsp.	each salt and pepper
10 oz.	can mushroom soup	¼ cup	grated Parmesan cheese

Combine all ingredients except cheese. Sprinkle it on top. Pour into casserole and bake at 325°F for 2 hours.

Sherwin and Sharon Petersen
S. H. Petersen, M.L.A.
Kelvington-Wadena
Saskatchewan

Main Course Casserole

1 lb.	ground beef	½	green pepper, chopped
3 tbsp.	shortening	2 tsp.	salt
2 cups	sliced raw potatoes	¼ tsp.	pepper
3	medium onions, sliced	1 tsp.	dried parsley
½ tsp.	garlic salt	2 cups	canned tomatoes
2 cups	chopped celery		

Preheat oven to 300°F.

Brown meat slightly in shortening. In a greased 2-quart casserole, put a layer of sliced potatoes. Add a layer of onions, then a layer of meat. Sprinkle meat with garlic salt. Combine celery and green pepper, add next. Season each layer with salt, pepper and dried parsley. Pour the canned tomatoes over all. Cover casserole and bake for 2½ hours. Uncover casserole during the last ½ hour of baking.

Harry Alger, M.L.A.
Highwood
Alberta

Wagon Wheel Ranch Chili

This recipe is one of our favourites during cattle-moving time every spring and fall, when we move to the community pasture 17 miles away. It's one of those where you throw in an extra can of beans and feed a few more!

4 tbsp.	fat	6 x 10 oz.	cans mushroom stems and pieces
2 cups	diced onion		
3-4	cloves garlic, crushed	6 x 19 oz.	cans tomatoes
8 lbs.	ground beef	6 x 19 oz.	cans pork and beans
	salt and pepper, to taste		flour

In a large pot or roaster heat fat, sauté onion and garlic. Add ground beef, salt and pepper to taste, and stir until nicely browned. Drain fat. Add mushrooms, tomatoes and pork and beans. Slowly bring to a boil, stirring constantly. Boil about 10 minutes. Thicken with flour to the thickness you like. I do not drain any of the juices from the mushrooms, tomatoes or beans. Serves from 30 to 40 people.

John and Gladys Drobot
John Drobot, M.L.A.
St. Paul
Alberta

Chili

3 lbs.	ground round	5	large Spanish onions, chopped OR 1 cup onion flakes
10 oz.	can mushrooms		
¾ cup	brown sugar		
1 tsp.	salt	3	stalks celery, finely chopped
	pepper, be generous	1-2	green peppers, chopped
1 tsp.	crushed chili, more if desired	2 x 19 oz.	cans baked beans OR home-made
1 tsp.	dry mustard		
¾ cup	ketchup	28 oz.	can tomatoes

Brown ground beef in large pot. Add remaining ingredients. Cook over low heat, covered, for 2 hours.

Hon. Brenda Robertson
Senator
New Brunswick

Rick's Very Favourite Sweet and Sour Meatballs

1	egg	½ cup	cornstarch
⅓	milk	1-2 tbsp.	corn oil
2	slices crumbled bread	10 oz.	can consommé
¼ cup	finely chopped onion	¼ cup	brown sugar
1 tsp.	salt	¼ cup	white vinegar
1½ lbs.	minced beef		

Mix egg into milk, add bread, onion and salt. Add beef, mix well, form into balls and roll in cornstarch. Brown meatballs in oil. Heat consommé, sugar and vinegar. After the meatballs are well browned lower the heat of pan to simmer, and add the sauce. Continue cooking for about 30 minutes, spooning sauce over 2 or 3 times. The meatballs will become glazed with the sauce, but watch carefully the last 5 minutes when it does begin to thicken. Serve with rice and a green vegetable. Serves 4-6.

Rick and Elizabeth Folk
Hon. Rick Folk, M.L.A.
Saskatoon-University
Saskatchewan

Beef Balls Tahiti

Meat Mixture:

1½ lbs.	ground chuck beef	½ cup	finely chopped or crushed walnuts (optional)
1 tsp.	salt		
½ tsp.	monosodium glutimate	4 tbsp.	milk
¼ tsp.	pepper	2 tbsp.	chopped onion or bottled onion flakes
2	small eggs		
1 cup	(lightly packed) soft bread crumbs (about 2 slices)		

Batter:

2	eggs	1 cup	unsifted flour
¾ cup	milk		

Sauce:

½ cup	vinegar or white wine	½ cup	vinegar or diluted lemon juice
2	beef soup cubes		
½ cup	boiling water	½ cup	soy sauce
1 tbsp.	cornstarch	1	green pepper, cut into squares
2 tbsp.	sugar		
½ cup	pineapple juice	1 cup	pineapple chunks

In a large mixing bowl, combine all meat mixture ingredients. Let stand about 10 minutes. Meanwhile, combine all batter ingredients in smaller bowl and beat smooth with a rotary beater. Shape meat mixture into about 28 or 30 balls ¾"-1-- diameter and drop a few at a time into batter.

Heat shortening or oil in a small pan. Use a 6" diameter pan with shortening 1" deep, heated to 375°F (cube of bread browns in 40 seconds). Lift meat balls from batter with a fork, drop into hot fat — about 4 at a time — and when bottom is golden, turn over to other side. Skim out into large frying pan with lid. When all are done, add to the meatballs the vinegar or wine and boiling water in which you have dissolved the beef soup cubes and simmer covered for 15 minutes.

Mix the cornstarch and sugar to a smooth paste in the pineapple juice and to them add the vinegar and soy sauce. Stir gently into meat balls until thickened. Add green pepper and pineapple chunks and simmer covered until green pepper is softened and hot, but still bright green.

Serve with fluffy rice.

Brian Lee, M.L.A.
Calgary Buffalo
Alberta

Porcupine Meat Balls

This is M.L.A.s "Steak"

½ cup	long-grain rice	1 tbsp.	minced onion
1-1½ lbs.	lean ground beef	10 oz.	can tomato soup
1 tsp.	salt	½	soup can water
½ tsp.	pepper		

Wash rice thoroughly if necessary. Combine all ingredients except soup and water. Shape into small balls.

Heat soup and water in pressure cooker. Drop meat balls into soup mixture. Close cover securely and place pressure regulator on vent pipe. Cook 10 minutes at 15 lbs. pressure. Remove from heat and let pressure drop of its own accord. Serves 5-6.

May be cooked in oven, if so, add more liquid.

Norm A. Weiss, M.L.A.
Lac La Biche/McMurray
Alberta

Carrot Meatballs

1 lb.	ground beef	¼ cup	milk
2	large carrots, shredded (1 cup)	1 tsp.	salt
		¼ tsp.	pepper
1	small onion, chopped (⅓ cup)	1 tsp.	oil
½ cup	bread crumbs	10 oz.	can beef gravy
1	egg		

Mix all ingredients, except oil and gravy. Shape into balls and brown in oil. Add gravy, cover and simmer for 15 minutes.

Optional: make your own gravy. Serve over noodles or rice. Serves 4.

Don and Kathleen Marmen
Don Marmen, M.L.A.
Madawaska Centre
New Brunswick

Cabbage Rolls Á La "Butch"

8	large cabbage leaves	1 tsp.	salt
1 lb.	ground beef	¼ tsp.	pepper
1 cup	cooked rice	pinch	garlic
¼ cup	chopped onions	14 oz.	can tomato sauce
1	egg, lightly beaten		

Boil cabbage leaves for a few minutes to soften the leaves. Mix beef, rice, onions, egg, salt, pepper and garlic with 2 tbsp. of sauce. Divide into 8 rolls and put into cabbage leaves. Hold cabbage with toothpicks or tie with thick sewing thread. Place in a casserole dish and add rest of sauce. Cover casserole and bake at low temperature 325°F, for 40 minutes. Serve with homemade buns, bread or rolls. Serves 4.

Roger (Butch) Wedge, M.L.A.
Bay du Vin
New Brunswick

Newfoundland Jiggs Dinner

3 lbs.	salt beef	1	med. turnip
1	med. head cabbage	6	med. potatoes
1 lb.	carrots	1 lb.	split peas

Soak salt beef in cold water overnight. Change water before putting on to cook. Cook for 2 hours. Add cabbage, carrots, turnip, cook for 10 minutes. Add potatoes, continue cooking for 25 minutes. See Peas Pudding, below, for use of split peas. Serves 6.

Peas Pudding

Soak peas in pudding bag with salt beef overnight. Cook same amount of time as meat. When mashing cooked peas add ¼ lb. (½ cup) butter, 1 tablespoon pepper and salt to taste. Serves 6.

Ray Baird, M.H.A.
Humber West
Newfoundland and Labrador

Ginger Ale Brisket

4-5 lb.	brisket	2 tbsp.	chili sauce
	salt, pepper, garlic powder,	2 tbsp.	soy sauce
	to taste	2 tbsp.	barbecue sauce
3	onions, sliced	10 oz.	can ginger ale
10 oz.	can kosher beef gravy		

Season brisket, with salt, pepper and garlic powder, the night before if possible. Preheat oven to 400°F. Mix soy sauce, chili sauce and barbecue sauce together. Brush on fat side of brisket. Place in open roasting pan. Add ginger ale. Bake for about 1½ hours. Remove from oven. Turn heat to 350°F. Add sliced onions and potatoes. Cover and bake 2 hours more, until tender. Take brisket out of sauce and keep warm for slicing. Pour sauce into pan and add can of gravy. Bring to a boil and serve over brisket or separately.

Jack and Evelyn Marshall
Hon. Jack Marshall
The Senate
Newfoundland and Labrador

Moose Swiss Steak

moose steaks	stewed tomatoes
seasoned flour	water
oil	seasoned pepper
onions	seasoned salt

The cut of meat used can be anything that you would use for a roast. Cut into steaks and tenderize by pounding the poorer cuts. Drench your meat in seasoned flour and brown in oil or shortening. Place in casserole or small roasting pan, cover with onions and pour over the stewed tomatoes. Also put a cup of water with the drippings in the pan the meat was browned in, stir getting as much of dripping as you can and pour this over meat. Season as you wish. I use seasoned pepper and seasoned salt. Cover and bake in 350°F oven for 1 hour.

Served with mashed potatoes and a green salad or cole slaw. Makes a wholesome delicious meal.

Bill and Julie Brewster
Bill Brewster, M.L.A.
Kluane
Yukon

Baked Stuffed Lobsters

8	lobsters, cooked		salt and pepper to taste
1 cup	margarine	2 cups	bread crumbs
2	large onions		
1 tsp.	savoury		

Remove lobster body from shells and set aside all meat and caviar. Cut tails in half from back, crack arms and claws and remove some of the shell.

Melt margaine in saucepan, dice onions. Add savoury, onions, salt, pepper and lobster meat from arms and body, also caviar. Add bread crumbs and mix together.

Stuff lobster bodies with dressing and heat in oven 350°F for 20 minutes, along with tails and claws.

Serve with melted butter with touch of lemon. Serves 6.

Hon. A. Brian Peckford, P.C., M.H.A.
Premier of Newfoundland and Labrador

Lobster Newburg

4 tbsp.	butter	½ tsp.	paprika
2 cups	boiled, diced lobster meat	3	egg yolks
¼ cup	dry sherry	1 cup	cream
			hot buttered toast

Melt butter in a double boiler over hot water. Add sherry. Cook gently for about 2 minutes. Add lobster meat, stir and cook. Add paprika. Beat together egg yolks and cream. Add to lobster mixture and cook, stirring, until mixture thickens. Season to taste. Serve at once on hot buttered toast.

Wilfred MacDonald, M.L.A.
Fifth Queens
Prince Edward Island

Lobster Casserole

⅔ cup	fine egg noodles	1	large cold pack of lobster, drained and chopped
½ cup	chopped onion		
1 cup	chopped celery	4 oz.	can shrimp and/or crab (optional)
½ cup	chopped green pepper		
10 oz.	can cream of mushroom soup		buttered bread or cracker crumbs
10 oz.	can mushrooms, drained white sauce (recipe follows)		

Cook egg noodles for 8 minutes until tender and drain. Sauté onions, celery and green pepper until tender. Combine cream of mushroom soup, mushrooms and white sauce. Add celery mixture, egg noodles and seafood. Pour into buttered casserole dish. Sprinkle buttered crumbs over top. Bake at 350°F for 50 minutes. Serves 10 and can be doubled easily for a crowd.

White Sauce:

¼ cup	butter	⅓ cup	Parmesan cheese
2-3 tbsp.	flour		salt, pepper to taste
1½-2 cups	milk		

Melt butter in saucepan over medium heat. Stir in flour. Gradually add milk. Cook, stirring regularly until mixture thickens and begins to bubble. Add cheese and seasoning.

Tom and Katherine McMillan
Hon. Tom McMillan, Q.C., M.P.
Hillsborough
Prince Edward Island

Lobster Thermidor

3 tbsp.	butter	½ cup	milk
2 cups	lobster meat	2 cups	thin cream
½ tsp.	onion	2-3 tbsp.	flour
10 oz.	can mushrooms	4 tbsp.	grated Cheddar cheese
½ cup	sherry or dry wine (optional)		

Melt butter and cook lobster in it for 5 minutes. Add onions, mushrooms, wine if used, milk and cream. Bring this to a slight boil. Thicken with flour and add cheese. Bake in an oven for 30 minutes at 350°F.

Serve in pastry shells with baked potato and salad.

Hon. Roddy Pratt, M.L.A.
Second Kings
Prince Edward Island

Lobster Supreme

1 lb.	fresh fish fillets		pepper, to taste
5 oz.	lobster	1¼ cups	milk
1	small tin lobster paste	1 tsp.	chopped parsley
2 tbsp.	butter	1 tsp.	chopped onion
3 tbsp.	flour	1 cup	bread crumbs
	salt, to taste		lemon slices and parsley

Cover the bottom of a casserole with fish fillets. Chop canned lobster into small pieces and combine with lobster juice and lobster paste. Spread this mixture over fillets. Cream together butter, flour, salt, pepper and milk. Add parsley and onion. Cook until thick and spread over the lobster mixture. Top with bread crumbs. Pat crumbs into the sauce. Bake for 40 minutes at 350°F.

Decorate with lemon slices and parsley.

A. A. (Joey) Fraser, M.L.A.
Third Kings
Prince Edward Island

Seafood Casserole

A combination of shellfish and finfish in a rich, cheese sauce. Everybody's favourite, especially these two New Brunswick families.

2 lbs.	one OR several of the following: scallops, lobster, haddock, crab, shrimp, cod	2	egg yolks
		1 cup	cereal cream OR milk
		1 cup	OR 4 oz. mushrooms, sliced
2 cups	water	1 tbsp.	butter
2	chicken bouillon cubes	⅛ tsp.	Worcestershire sauce
6 tbsp.	butter	pinch	cayenne papper
6 tbsp.	flour	3 cups	bread cubes
1 cup	OR ¼ lb. grated Cheddar cheese	2 tbsp.	butter, melted

If frozen, thaw fish overnight in the refrigerator. If time is short, wrap in a plastic bag and place under cold, running water for an hour or 2. If scallops or shrimps are "individually quick frozen" there is no need to thaw. Reserve liquid if canned fish is used. Check for bits of shell. Chop lobster meat into bite-sized pieces and remove cartilage from the claw meat. Cut fillets into cubes.

Bring water to the boil. Add raw fish and simmer 3 or 4 minutes. Remove fish and dissolve cubes in poaching water. In saucepan make roux of butter and flour. Gradually beat in the 2 cups of hot liquid. Continue to stir and cook until sauce thickens. Add cheese, cook and stir until well blended. Remove from the heat. Combine egg yolks and cream, beat with a fork and add slowly to the sauce while stirring vigorously.

Wash and slice mushrooms; cook in 1 tablespoon butter. Add the mushrooms, Worcestershire sauce, cayenne pepper and shellfish to the sauce. Taste sauce carefully and salt if required. Preheat oven to 450°F. Pour mixture into 1½-quart, lightly greased casserole or individual scallop shells or casseroles. Toss bread cubes in melted butter and sprinkle over top. Bake in the oven until bread cubes are golden, approximately 15 minutes. Serves 8.

Hon. Yvon R. Poitras, M.L.A.
Restigouche West
New Brunswick
and
Hon. Leslie I. Hull, M.L.A.
York South
New Brunswick

Seafood Casserole

1 lb.	fresh haddock fillets	6 tbsp.	butter
1 lb.	fresh scallops	10 oz.	can cream of mushroom soup
4 cups	homogenized milk		
14 oz.	can lobster (reserve juice)	½ cup	fresh mushrooms, sautéed in butter
7 oz.	can shrimp		
½ cup	flour	1⅓ cups	breadcrumbs, sautéed in butter

Chop fish and scallops into bite-sized pieces and simmer in milk for 8 minutes. Save milk for use in sauce. Combine fish and shellfish.

Cook flour and butter together a few minutes before adding milk, juice from lobster and the soup. Cook until thickened.

Butter a large casserole and layer sauce, seafood mixture to which mushrooms are added, and rice, beginning and ending with sauce. Sprinkle bread crumbs on top and bake at 325°F for 45 minutes. Serves 12.

Serve with a tossed green salad and crusty French bread.

Hon. Harold Fanjoy, M.L.A.
Kings Centre
New Brunswick

Seafood Casserole

1 lb.	scallops (boil 1 minute and quarter)	3 cups	milk
		1 cup	juice from seafood mixture
2 x 4.5 oz.	cans crabs		salt and pepper
1 lb.	cooked lobster	3 stalks	celery, finely chopped
1 lb.	shrimps	1	small onion, finely chopped
¼ cup	flour		
1 lb.	mozzarella cheese		

Mix seafoods together. Make sauce by heating together next 5 ingredients. Sauté celery and onion, and add to sauce. Combine seafood and sauce and bake in open casserole at 350°F for about 20 minutes.

Gerald and Aurore Comeau
Gerald Comeau, M.P.
South West Nova
Nova Scotia

Seafood Casserole

3 tbsp.	butter		1 lb.	scallops
2 tbsp.	flour		2	hard-boiled eggs
1¼ cups	milk		½ cup	chopped onions
10 oz.	can mushroom soup		½ cup	chopped green pepper
10 oz.	can whole mushrooms		½ cup	chopped celery
1 lb.	haddock OR			bread crumbs
14 oz.	can lobster			

Prepare white sauce with first 3 ingredients. Stir in soup and mushrooms. Combine remaining ingredients, except crumbs, stir in sauce and put in casserole dish. Cover with bread crumbs. Bake in 350°F oven for about 40 minutes.

Hon. Leone Bagnall, M.L.A.
First Queens
Prince Edward Island

Seafood Casserole

½ lb.	butter		2 x 10 oz.	cans mushrooms
1 cup	flour			sherry
4 cups	milk			grated cheese, optional
1½ tsp.	salt		1½ cups	frozen peas
½ tsp.	pepper		1½ lbs.	lobster
	paprika		1½ lbs.	shrimp
	Worcestershire sauce		1½ lbs.	haddock fillets
10 oz.	can cream of mushroom soup		½ lbs.	crab

Make white sauce using the first 7 ingredients. Add cream of mushrooms soup, mushrooms, sherry, cheese and peas.

Cook seafood, flake fillets, and add to sauce. Heat in 325°F oven until hot. Do not boil.

Freezes beatifully but do not heat before freezing. Remove from freezer up to 24 hours and thaw, then heat at 325°F for 45 minutes. Serves 12.

Tom and Bernadette McInnis
Hon. Thomas J. McInnis, M.L.A
Halifax Eastern Shore
Nova Scotia

Seafood Supreme

4 tbsp.	chopped green pepper	½ tsp.	salt
2 tbsp.	chopped green onion	½ tsp.	Worcestershire sauce
1 cup	chopped celery	½ tsp.	pepper
1 cup	crab meat	1 cup	mayonnaise
1 cup	cooked shrimp		crushed potato chips for
1 cup	cold cooked rice		topping
10 oz.	pkg. frozen peas		

Mix together all ingredients, except potato chips, in a large bowl. Put into a greased casserole. Cover with crushed potato chips. Bake at 325°F for 30 minutes. Serves 4-6.

Len and Alice Gustafson
Len Gustafson, M.P.
Assiniboia
Saskatchewan

Salmon or Crab Casserole

12 oz.	salmon OR crab	2 tbsp.	butter
1 cup	cooked Minute Rice	10 oz.	can cream of mushroom
½ cup	chopped onion		soup
2 tbsp.	green pepper	⅔ cup	milk
		1¾ cups	crushed potato chips

Flake fish and combine with rice. Cook onion and green pepper in butter until tender and add to fish mixture. Mix soup and liquid until smooth. Spread half of chips in greased casserole and cover with alternate layers of fish and soup. Bake at 350°F for 30 minutes.

Hon. Ron Dawe, M.H.A.
St. George's
Newfoundland and Labrador

Crab Soufflé

4	slices white bread, cubed	4	slices white bread
2 cups	crab meat	4	eggs
½ cup	mayonnaise	3 cups	milk
1	medium onion, chopped	10 oz.	can cream of mushroom soup
1 cup	chopped celery		
1	medium green pepper, chopped	¾ cup	shredded cheese paprika

Arrange cubed bread in bottom of deep 7" x 11" baking dish. Fold crab, mayonnaise, onion, celery, green pepper and spoon over cubes.

Trim crusts from remaining bread slices and cover mixture. Beat eggs and milk together and pour over bread. Cover and chill for 8 hours. (I make it the day before and leave it overnight).

Heat oven to 325°F. Remove cover and bake for 15 minutes. Remove from oven and spread mushroom soup over bread, top with grated cheese and a sprinkle of paprika.

Bake for 1 hour.

Barbara J. Sparrow, M.P.
Calgary South
Alberta

Baked Scallops in the Shell

1 lb.	scallops	4 tsp.	dry bread crumbs
	salt and pepper	4 tsp.	melted butter
4 tbsp.	heavy cream		

Place scallops on 4 greased scallop shells. Add 1 tbsp. cream to each shell. Sprinkle with salt and pepper, cover with dry bread crumbs and drizzle with melted butter. Bake at 450°F for 20 minutes. Serves 4.

Hon. Albert Fogarty, M.L.A.
First Kings
Prince Edward Island

Poor Man's Coquille St. Jacques

1 cup	stone wheat crackers, crushed		garlic powder, to taste
			ground pepper, to taste
2 tbsp.	butter OR margarine, melted	1 lb.	scallops
½ tsp.	lemon juice		mozzarella cheese slices
	tarragon, to taste		

Preheat oven to 425°F for 15 minutes. Crush cracker crumbs, add butter, lemon juice and spices. Roll scallops in mixture. Grease scallop shells or shallow pan. Add scallops, cover with cheese slices. Bake for 15 minutes or, if you like your scallops well-done, bake 10 minutes before adding cheese and 10 minutes with the cheese.

Howard E. Crosby, Q.C., M.P.
Halifax West
Nova Scotia

Taylor's Curried Shrimp

2 tbsp.	butter	¼ tsp.	ground ginger
2 tbsp.	flour	1 cup	milk
¼ tsp.	salt	1	egg yolk, slightly beaten
	few grains pepper	2 cups	cleaned, cooked shrimp
1 tsp.	curry powder		

Melt butter in top of double boiler. Add flour, salt, pepper, curry powder and ginger. Blend well. Gradually pour on milk. Boil 2 minutes. Cook 15 minutes in double boiler. If necessary thin with a little extra milk. Just before serving add 1 slightly beaten egg yolk. Heat shrimp in above mixture and serve with hot boiled rice and chutney. Serves 4.

James Taylor, Q.C., M.P.P.
Prince Edward-Lennox
Ontario

Deep-Fried Shrimp

	oil, for deep-frying		raw, shelled shrimp

Tempura batter:

1 cup	ice-cold water	¼ tsp.	salt
1	egg	1 cup	unsifted cake flour
¼ tsp.	baking soda	½ cup	unsifted cake flour

In a deep-frying pan heat 1½"-2" of salad oil to 375°F on deep-frying thermometer. Meanwhile wipe shrimp dry and prepare tempura batter. In a bowl combine ice-cold water, egg, soda and salt. Beat slightly. Add 1 cup cake-flour, mix until just blended. Batter will be lumpy. Sprinkle ½ cup cake flour over top of batter. Stir slightly, 1 or 2 strokes. Most of the flour should be floating on top of batter. Fill a larger bowl half full of ice; set bowl of batter in it to keep batter cold while you dip and cook shrimp. Dip shrimp in batter and let excess drip off before adding to hot oil. Fry until golden brown, 8-10 minutes, drain on paper towels and serve with your favourite sauce.

Calvin and Marjorie Glauser
Calvin Glauser, M.L.A.
Saskatoon Mayfair
Saskatchewan

Barbecued Salmon

1	salmon, cut in half lengthwise		brown sugar
			pickling salt

Sprinkle salmon lightly with pickling salt on inside portion of the halves. Follow this with a liberal (not conservative) layer of brown sugar. Place directly on barbecue grill scale-side down and cook approximately 20-25 minutes depending on the size of the salmon. Salmon is done when fat has percolated through the flesh and condensed on the surface as white globs. Delicious with a green salad and rice.

Of course a yearly fishing trip to B.C. is needed to replenish salmon supply.

Paul Gagnon, M.P.
Calgary North
Alberta

Barbecued Salmon Marinade

For each five pounds of salmon, mix thoroughly:

½-¾ cup	rye whisky	1 tsp.	powdered garlic
¾ cup	vegetable oil	dash	pepper
4 tbsp.	demerara brown sugar		

Place portion-sized pieces of filleted salmon in deep container, pour mixture over salmon and set aside a minimum of 4 hours or up to 24 hours.

Place salmon, skin side down, on barbecue and cover with tin foil.

Cook 5-10 minutes maximum.

Mary Collins, M.P.
Capilano
British Columbia

Broiled Salmon Steaks with Mustard Sauce

2	salmon steaks, about ¾" thick	3 tbsp.	melted butter
		2 tbsp.	lemon juice

Heat broiler. Brush salmon steaks with melted butter and lemon juice. Broil 5-6 minutes on each side, basting with butter and juice when turning. Serve with hot mustard sauce.

Mustard Sauce:

2 tbsp.	white wine	1 tbsp.	fresh dill OR 1 tsp. dried
2 tbsp.	Dijon mustard		

Heat wine in small sauté pan over high heat. Stir in mustard and cook until slightly thickened, 2-3 minutes. Add dill and serve.

Hon. Jack B. Murta, P.C., M.P.
Lisgar
Manitoba

Salmon Pie

3 cups	mashed potatoes	2 cups	milk
8 oz.	can of salmon	½ cup	grated cheese
3 tbsp.	butter	1 cup	crumbs OR crushed
1	medium onion, chopped		cornflakes
3 tbsp.	flour		

Line a buttered dish with mashed potatoes. Add chunked salmon. Melt butter in a pan and fry onions. Blend flour into the butter and onions. Add milk very gradually. Add grated cheese and cook on top of stove until smooth. Pour over mashed potatoes and salmon. Sprinkle crumbs on top. Bake at 350°F for 30 minutes.

Sid and Gerri Dutchak and family
Hon. S. P. Dutchak, M.L.A.
Prince Albert - Duck Lake
Saskatchewan

Baked Cod Tongues

24	cod tongues	2 tbsp.	salt
1 cup	milk	1 cup	bread crumbs

Wipe tongues with damp cloth. Soak 10 minutes in milk to which salt has been added. Drain and roll in dry bread crumbs. Place on an oiled sheet and bake in a hot oven, 450°F, for 10 minutes. Serve with tartar sauce.

Luke Woodrow, M.H.A.
Bay of Islands
Newfoundland and Labrador

Flipper Pie

Flippers are hard to come by these days.

	seal flippers (the forepaws)	2 or 3	onions, peeled and diced
	cold water	14 oz.	tin cranberry jelly
1 tbsp.	baking soda		pastry to cover the flippers
	flour		OR
	margarine		parsley and lemon, optional
1	tin beef gravy		

The flippers of a young seal are the most tender and tasty. Soak them in cold water containing the baking soda for 1 to 2 hours as this turns the fat snow white. With a razor, remove every bit of the fat, otherwise the dish will have a disagreeable, oily, fishy taste.

Preheat the oven to 400°F.

Cut the flippers in half at the round knuckle bone and roll them in the flour. In an iron skillet containing plenty of margarine brown the flippers about 5 to 10 minutes, being careful not to burn. Remove the flippers to a roasting pan.

To the margarine in the skillet add flour for the gravy. Add the beef gravy, water and additional flour until the gravy is the right consistency; it should be quite thick. The best way to add additional flour so as to prevent lumps is with a fine sifter.

Stir in the cranberry jelly and the onions and pour the gravy over the flippers. Add water, if necessary, to submerge the flippers in the gravy. Cover the pan and roast for about 1¼ hours. Remove briefly from the heat, turn the flippers over and return to the oven for about another 45 minutes, or until the meat starts to leave the bone.

After the dish has cooled, chill overnight in the refrigerator. Skim off any remaining fat. This is the secret of preparing flippers: the total elimination of all fat.

When ready to serve, cover the flippers with pastry, reheat and serve. As an alternative to making a pie, the flippers can be served with parsley and lemon.

John and Jane Crosbie
Hon. John Crosbie, P.C., M.P.
St. John's West
Newfoundland and Labrador

Cod Fillets with Cheese Sauce

1½ lbs.	fresh cod fillets	⅓ cup	grated cheese
2 tbsp.	butter	½ tsp.	powdered mustard
3 tbsp.	flour	¼ tsp.	salt
1 cup	hot milk		

Put fillets in baking dish. Melt butter, remove saucepan from heat and add flour. Mix well. Add hot milk, cheese, mustard and salt. Mix until cheese is melted. Cook 5 minutes. Pour over fish and place in oven at 500°F for 10-20 minutes.

Ida Reid, M.H.A.
Twillingate
Newfoundland and Labrador

Codfish Cakes

2	onions, chopped	¼ tsp.	pepper
2 cups	cooked salt codfish, boned	1	egg, well beaten
	and shredded	½ cup	fine bread crumbs, or
6-8	cooked potatoes		cornflake crumbs
3-4	cooked parsnips		

Cool onions in a very small amount of water. Mash together the fish, potatoes and parsnips. Add the onions and water in which they were cooked. Season. Add beaten egg and combine well. Form into cakes; roll in crumbs. Fry in rendered pork fat.

Excellent when made smaller and used as hors d'oeuvres. Freezes well.

Hon. H. W. House, M.H.A.
Humber Valley
Newfoundland and Labrador

Hickey's Fish Rolls

Fish Rolls:

2 lbs.	fresh cod fillets, cooked and flaked	1 tsp.	salt
		1 tsp.	paprika
¼ cup	finely chopped onion	16	large cabbage leaves, blanched for 3 minutes
1 cup	long grain rice, cooked		

Secret Sauce — Step 1:

¼ cup	butter	2 tsp.	sugar
1½ oz.	can tomato paste	6	peppercorns
7½ oz.	can tomato sauce	1	bay leaf
¼ cup	lemon juice	2 cups	water

Secret Sauce — Step 2:

3 tbsp.	chopped onion	3 tbsp.	flour
3 tbsp.	butter	1 tsp.	salt

Combine fish, onions, rice and seasonings. Use ⅓ cup per roll. Fill each cabbage leaf and fold sides to form package. Secure with toothpicks.

Prepare Secret Sauce — Step 1: Melt butter and add remaining ingredients. Bring to boiling point. Reduce heat. Place rolls in sauce. Cover and simmer for 15 minutes. Remove from sauce, remove toothpicks and keep rolls warm. Reserve sauce.

Prepare Secret Sauce — Step 2: Fry onions in melted butter. Add flour and salt and mix to form a paste. Spoon into reserved tomato sauce, cook until thickened. Serve over hot fish rolls. Serves 6.

Hon. T. V. Hickey, M.H.A.
St. John's East Extern
Newfoundland and Labrador

Jim McGrath's Famous Saltfish Dish

1	medium salt codfish		pepper
2	medium onions, chopped		Worcestershire sauce
	vegetable oil	2 tbsp.	brown sugar
	tomato paste	2	tomatoes
	garlic		

Skin 1 medium-sized salt codfish and soak it in water for 24 hours, then boil it for 30 minutes.

Sauté onions in oil. Place in casserole dish and place boiled fish in dish. Cover with tomato paste seasoned with garlic, pepper, Worcestershire sauce and brown sugar. Add freshly cut tomatoes. Cover with aluminum foil and bake for 30 minutes at 350°F. Serve with rice or mashed potatoes and ENJOY!

Hon. James A. McGrath, P.C., M.P.
St. John's East
Newfoundland

Lunenburg Casserole Delicacy with Mushroom Sauce

Although its origin is lost in antiquity, this recipe has been a family favourite for many years. I'm sure your readers will enjoy this Maritime delicacy!

½ cup	dry sherry	2 lbs.	haddock, sole OR cod
2 x 10 oz.	cans mushroom soup	1 cup	fresh mushrooms
½ tsp.	ginger powder	1 cup	shrimp
½ tsp.	salt	½ tsp.	Accent

To make sauce, combine sherry, soup, ginger powder, salt and Accent.

Spread ½ the sauce mixture evenly in baking dish. Fold fillets of fish and pack nicely in the sauce. Add cut mushrooms. Top with shrimp and add rest of sauce.

Bake at 375°F for 45 minutes or until well done. Serves 8 people.

NOTE: This may be assembled ahead and refrigerated until time to bake.

Lloyd R. Crouse, M.P.
South Shore
Nova Scotia

Halibut Royale

3 tbsp.	lemon juice		½ cup	chopped onion
1 tsp.	salt		2 tbsp.	butter or margarine
½ tsp.	paprika		6	green pepper strips
6	halibut steaks			

In shallow dish combine lemon juice, salt and paprika. Add halibut and marinate for 1 hour, turning steaks after first ½ hour.

Cook chopped onion in butter until tender but not brown.

Place steaks in greased 10" x 6" baking dish. Top with green pepper strips, and sprinkle with cooked onion. Bake in very hot oven, 450°F, about 40 minutes or until fish flakes easily. Serves 6.

Joe and Belle Price
Joe Price, M.P.
Burin-St. George's
Newfoundland and Labrador

Barbecued Halibut Sticks

1 tsp.	salt		1½-2 lbs.	halibut steaks, ½" thick
1	clove garlic, finely chopped			grated Parmesan cheese
½ cup	salad oil		1 cup	dry bread crumbs

Combine salt, garlic and oil; let stand. Cut fish into 1" x 2" sticks. Place fish in oil mixture for 1 minute. Remove from oil. Sprinkle on all sides with cheese; roll in bread crumbs. Place on greased cookie sheet. Bake at 450°F for 12 minutes or until brown. Serve plain or with tartar sauce. Serves 4.

Fred R. Stagg, M.H.A.
Stephenville
Newfoundland and Labrador

Fried Haddock
Halibut, or Boston Bluefish

	fish fillets		melted butter and shortening
1	egg	1 cup	hot water
½ cup	evaporated milk	½ tsp.	salt
½ tsp.	salt		butter size of walnuts
	flour	dash	pepper
	cracker crumbs	1	large onion, sliced

Cut fish fillets to desired size and sprinkle with salt. Beat together egg, undiluted evaporated milk and salt. Roll fish in flour, dip in egg and milk mixture, then roll again in very fine cracker crumbs. Fry in ¼" hot melted butter and vegetable shortening until golden brown, remove from pan, place where it will keep hot until ready to serve. To the pan in which fish has been fried, add hot water, salt, butter, pepper, and onion. Cook until onion is tender, then add flour mixed with water to thicken. Serve gravy separately from fish. Serve with mashed potatoes and green peas.

Hon. James N. Tucker, M.L.A.
Charlotte-Fundy
New Brunswick

Dėvilled Haddock

¼ lb.	mushrooms	1 tbsp.	Worcestershire sauce
	butter	2 tbsp.	snipped parsley
2 cups	cream sauce	2 cups	cooked fish
	salt and pepper	3	slices bread, crumbled
2 tbsp.	dry mustard		

Fry mushrooms in butter and mix with sauce. Add seasonings. Put fish into casserole and pour sauce over it. Brown bread crumbs in butter and sprinkle on top. Bake ½ hour at 350°F.

The Hon. John Buchanan, P.C., M.L.A.
Premier of Nova Scotia

Stuffed Haddock with Lobster Newburg

Stuffed Haddock:

3	slices white bread, crusts removed	1 cup	cooked lobster meat, cubed
		2 lbs.	haddock fillets (6-8)
2 tbsp.	dry sherry or wine	2 tbsp.	melted butter
1 tbsp.	grated Cheddar cheese	½ cup	milk
⅛ tsp.	salt		salt

Newburg Sauce:

4 tbsp.	butter	1 tsp.	salt
2 tbsp.	flour	1 cup	cooked lobster meat, cubed
1 cup	milk	2 tbsp.	dry sherry or wine
1 cup	heavy cream		

Preheat oven to 350°F and prepare haddock. Crumble bread with sherry, cheese, salt and lobster. Place some mixture at 1 end of fillet, roll up and fasten with toothpick. Put in flat baking dish. Pour butter and milk over fillets and sprinkle with salt. Bake uncovered for 25 minutes.

To prepare sauce, melt 2 tbsp. butter. Remove from heat and blend in flour. Gradually stir in combined milk and cream. Bring to boil, stirring constantly until smooth and thickened. Add salt. Melt remaining 2 tbsp. butter in skillet. Add lobster and sherry. Cook slowly, about 5 minutes, until liquid is absorbed. Add lobster to sauce mixture.

Serve rolled fillets topped with sauce. Serves 6-8.

NOTE: If haddock is not available, sole or any other whitefish may be substituted.

Alex and Carmel McIntosh
Alex McIntosh, M.L.A.
Yarmouth
Nova Scotia

Barbecued Mackerel

6	mackerel fillets		chopped onions
2	lemons, sliced		salt and pepper
	butter		

Wrap mackerel fillets separately in foil with lemon slice, dot of butter, onion, salt and pepper. Barbecue for 20 minutes — 10 minutes on each side. Serve with hash browns, see recipe below.

Hash Browns

1 lb.	pkg. frozen hash browns	1 cup	grated cheese
10 oz.	can mushroom soup	1	chopped onion
1 cup	sour cream		

Mix all ingredients together and bake for 1 hour at 350°F.

Hon. Frederick L. Driscoll, M.L.A.
Third Queens
Prince Edward Island

Tuna Cashew Casserole

3 oz.	jar Chow Mein Noodles	¼ lb.	cashew nuts
10 oz.	can cream of mushroom soup	1 cup	finely diced celery
		¼ cup	minced onion
¼ cup	water	dash	pepper and salt
6.5 oz.	can chunky tuna (1 cup)		

Put aside ¼ cup noodles. Combine all ingredients. Bake at 325°F for 40 minutes. Sprinkle reserved noodles on top.

Hon. R. Laird Stirling, M.L.A.
Dartmouth North
Nova Scotia

Sole Amandine

At the insistence of my colleague, the Minister of Fisheries, who is attempting to increase the export of Nova Scotia fish, I offer the following recipe.

14 oz.	pkg. individually frozen fillets of sole	2 tbsp.	butter
2 tbsp.	melted butter	¼ cup	blanched almonds
½ tsp.	salt	1 tbsp.	lemon juice
	paprika		parsley

Place fillets in a single layer on a well-greased ovenproof platter. Brush fillets with melted butter. Broil 4" from source of heat for about 10 minutes or until fish flakes easily when tested with a fork. Sprinkle cooked fillets with salt and paprika. While fillets cook, make sauce by melting remaining butter over low heat, add nuts and cook slowly until almonds are golden. Stir in lemon juice. Pour sauce over cooked fillets. Garnish with parsley. Serves 3.

Hon. Gerald Sheehy, D.V.M., M.L.A.
Annapolis East
Nova Scotia

Sole Fillets Viennese

16 oz.	frozen sole fillets	1 tbsp.	flour
½ tsp.	salt	¾ cup	diced cucumber
2 tsp.	lemon juice	6	slices bacon, diced and fried crisp
1 cup	sour cream		
2 tsp.	prepared mustard few grains salt	¼ cup	shredded Parmesan cheese

Thaw fish fillets following package directions. Sprinkle fish evenly with ½ tsp. salt. Arrange half fish fillets in buttered, shallow casserole. Drizzle with lemon juice.

Beat together the sour cream, prepared mustard, few grains salt and flour.

Cover fish fillets with ½ the sour cream mixture, ¼ cup of cucumber and ½ the bacon. Repeat with remaining fish fillets and sour cream mixture, cucumber and bacon. Top with Parmesan cheese.

Bake at 375°F for 20 minutes or until fish flakes easily when tested with a fork.

Graham L. Harle, M.L.A.
Stettler
Alberta

Sweet and Sour Lake Perch

2	eggs	14 oz.	can pineapple tidbits
2 tbsp.	flour		cornstarch
1 tsp.	salt	½ cup	brown sugar
¼ tsp.	pepper	3 tbsp.	soy sauce
2 lbs.	perch fillets, cut into pieces	½ cup	vinegar
½ cup	oil	4	stalks celery
2	cubes chicken bouillon,	1	tomato
	dissolved in 1 cup water	1	red pepper (or green)

Beat eggs, flour, salt and pepper together. Dip fish pieces in egg batter and deep-fry in oil. Remove and drain. Combine bouillon, pineapple tidbits and juice, boil for 5 minutes. Mix cornstarch, sugar, soy sauce, vinegar and add to pineapple mixture. Add celery. Cook until thickened. Pour sweet and sour sauce over fish, bake in oven for ½ hour at 350°F. Garnish with tomato and pepper 15 minutes before end of cooking.

Kenneth and Jeannine Kowalski
Kenneth R. Kowalski, M.L.A.
Barrhead
Alberta

Baked Salt Turbot

A sweet white wine complements this wonderful Newfoundland specialty.

1 lb.	salt turbot		butter
	parsley flakes	1	small finely chopped onion
	pepper	1	lemon, cut into wedges
	savory		

Place the salt turbot in a buttered baking dish. Sprinkle generously with parsley and lightly with pepper and savory. Top with 2 or 3 thin layers of butter, diced onion and lemon wedges. Cover the dish with aluminum foil and bake in preheated 350°F oven for 1 to 1¼ hours, basting occasionally.

Serve with boiled potatoes, hot buttered corn and broccoli or spinach.

Tom Rideout, M.H.A.
Biae Verte-White Bay
Newfoundland and Labrador

Baked Whitefish and Wild Rice

¼ cup	butter		½ cup	bread crumbs
1	onion		2 tbsp.	dry sherry
1 cup	mushrooms		1½ cups	cereal cream
½ cup	celery		2 cups	cooked whitefish
2 tbsp.	parsley		1 cup	crab meat
½ cup	wild rice		½ cup	shrimp
½ cup	white rice		1 tsp.	lemon juice
1 tsp.	salt		½ cup	slivered almonds
1 tsp.	black pepper			Cheddar cheese, grated
dash	dash of Tabasco sauce			

In a large skillet melt butter, add minced onion, chopped mushrooms, chopped celery, minced parsley and sauté for 4-5 minutes.

In 2 saucepans, simmer wild rice with 2 cups of water and white rice with 1 cup of water until tender. The wild rice will take about 40 minutes, while the white rice will take about 25 minutes.

To the onion mixture, add salt, pepper, Tabasco, fine dry bread crumbs, dry sherry and cereal cream. Toss well.

In a bowl, combine flaked whitefish, crab meat and shrimp. Drizzle with fresh lemon juice.

In a deep, buttered, baking dish, layer in the rice and fish mixtures ending with a layer of rice.

Top with slivered almonds, grated Cheddar cheese and bake at 350°F for 35-45 minutes.

Let cool for 10 minutes then garnish with lemon wedges, parsley or watercress and serve.

Dave Nickerson, M.P.
Western Arctic
North West Territories

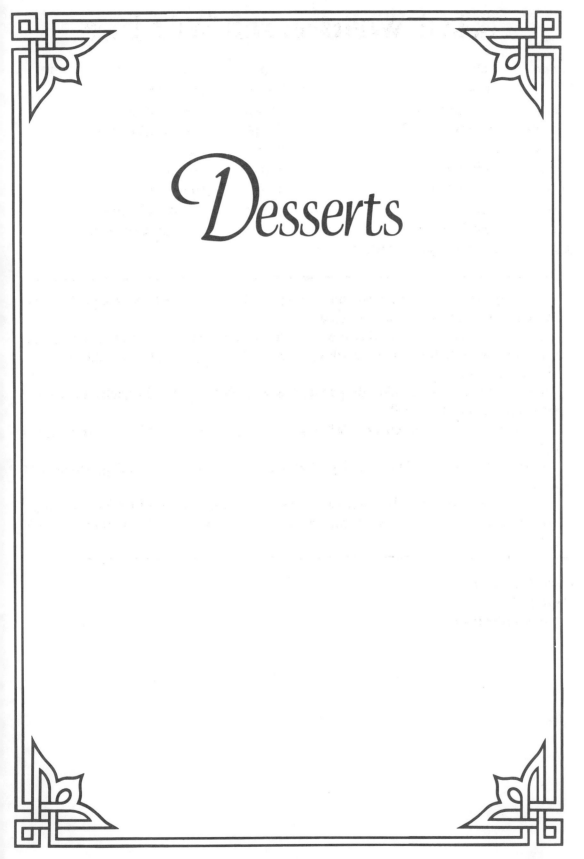

Desserts

Lemon Pie

I believe that everyone will enjoy my favourite recipe for lemon pie , and I am happy to enclose it for you. It comes from my mother, Mrs. Vera Davis.

3	egg yolks	1 tsp.	hot water
	rind and juice of 1 lemon	1 tsp.	butter, approximately
½ cup	sugar	3	egg whites
		½ cup	sugar

Combine first 5 ingredients. Boil together until thick, stirring constantly. Then take 3 egg whites and beat until stiff. Add ½ cup sugar and beat until it gets like meringue.

Fold whites and the custard together, carefully, and put in a pre-cooked pie shell. Brown lightly under broiler, very carefully.

Hon. William G. Davis, P.C., Q.C., M.P.P.
Premier of Ontario

Lemon Pear Pie

1 cup	sugar	¼ cup	lemon juice
1	egg, beaten	1 tbsp.	butter
1 tsp.	grated lemon rind	2 x 14 oz.	cans pears, drained
1½ tbsp.	cornstarch		pastry for 2-crust pie

Combine ingredients, except pears, and cook slowly over low heat stirring constantly until mixture thickens. Cool slightly. Line a 9" pie plate with pastry. Place pears in unbaked shell. Pour lemon mixture over top. Arrange lattice strips on top.

Bake 400°F for 35-40 minutes.

Ross and Ruth Belsher
Ross Belsher, M.P.
Fraser Valley East
British Columbia

Lemon Cheese/Butter

This spread is delicious on toast and it makes a great filling for tart shells.

¼ cup	butter		rind of 2 lemons, grated
2 cups	sugar	6	large OR 7 small eggs
	juice of 3 lemons		

Melt butter and sugar in top of double boiler or in a heavy pot.
Add lemon juice, grated rind and well-beaten eggs.
Cook, stirring constantly, until thick.
Makes 1 quart.

Gram's Pie Crust

This is a recipe that my mother-in-law gave me several years ago. I tell my friends that you could walk on this dough for a week and never have tough pastry.

¼ cup	butter, softened	3 cups	flour
½ lb.	lard, softened	½ cup	cold water
1 tsp.	salt		

Beat butter, lard and salt with a mixer or spatula until creamy. Add flour and cold water. Knead until smooth. Roll out on floured surface.

Al and Joyce Adair
Hon. Al Adair, M.L.A.
Peace River
Alberta

Apple and Cream Pie

1	unbaked 9" pie crust	3 tbsp.	flour
4	med. cooking apples, peeled and thinly sliced	1 tsp.	cinnamon
		1 tsp.	vanilla
1 cup	whipping cream	¼ tsp.	nutmeg
1 cup	sugar	⅛ tsp.	salt
1	egg	¾ cup	coarsely chopped walnuts

Place sliced apples in unbaked pie crust. Mix thoroughly the cream, sugar, egg, flour and seasonings. Pour over apples and sprinkle top with walnuts. Bake for 10 minutes at 450°F, reduce heat to 350°F. Bake until apples are tender, 35-40 minutes longer.

Albert G. Cooper, M.P.
Peace River
Alberta

Blue Grape Pie

A mouth-watering recipe using Ontario grapes

2½ cups	blue grapes	1 tbsp.	flour
1	egg	1 tbsp.	soft butter
1 cup	sugar		pastry
pinch	salt		

Wash, drain and stem grapes. Slip off the skins and simmer the pulp for about 5 minutes. Press pulp through sieve to remove seeds and make up measure of the pulp to ¾ cup, with cold water. Combine with skins. Beat the egg, add sugar, salt and flour. Add the grapes and mix in the soft butter. Line a pie plate with pastry, turn in the grape mixture. Cover with lattice strips of pastry if desired. Cook at 450°F for 10 minutes, then 375°F until pastry is cooked, about 30-35 minutes.

Doug and Kay Kennedy
Doug Kennedy, M.P.P.
Mississauga South
Ontario

Light 'N' Fruity Strawberry Pie

2	envelopes Dream Whip Dessert Topping Mix	1 cup	diced fresh strawberries OR 15 oz. pkg. frozen
3 oz.	pkg. strawberry Jell-o (85 g)		strawberries (425 g),
⅔ cup	boiling water		thawed and drained
2 cups	ice cubes	1	baked 9" graham wafer crumb crust, cooled

Prepare dessert topping mixes as directed on package. Dissolve jelly powder in boiling water. Add ice cubes and stir constantly until jelly starts to thicken, about 2 to 3 minutes. Remove any unmelted ice. Add prepared dessert topping to jelly and beat with electric mixer until well blended. Fold in fruit. Spoon into crust. Chill 3 hours. Garnish if desired.

Al Hiebert, M.L.A.
Edmonton Gold Bar
Alberta

Frozen Strawberry Pie

1½ cups	vanilla wafer crumbs	1 cup	granulated sugar
½ cup	chopped nuts	1	egg white
½ cup	melted butter	1 cup	dairy sour cream
1½ cups	sliced fresh strawberries		

Combine crumbs, nuts and butter in a small bowl and blend thoroughly. Press into bottom and sides of a 10" pie plate. Bake 8-10 minutes at 350°F. Cool. Combine strawberries, sugar and egg white in large bowl of mixer. Beat on medium high until soft peaks form. Gently fold in sour cream, mound into crust and freeze until firm. To serve let stand at room temperature until almost thawed.

Gordon and Doris Towers
Gordon Towers, M.P.
Red Deer
Alberta

Tory Ice Cream Pie

½ cup	coconut	⅔ cup	brown sugar
2 cups	crushed cornflakes	1 quart	vanilla ice cream
½ cup	chopped nuts	1	can fruit, drained, OR fresh
⅓ cup	butter		fruit in season

Combine coconut, cornflakes, and nuts. Melt butter and add brown sugar. Melt together until sugar dissolves. Add to cornflakes mixture and combine well.

Spray a 9½" pie plate with Pam. Press mixture into the shape of the dish and chill. Pour softened ice cream into pie mould, chill.

This can be made ahead of time and kept in freezer. Just before serving, pour drained fruit over the pie. Serves 6.

Bill and Joan Payne
Hon. Bill Payne, M.L.A.
Calgary Fish Creek
Alberta

Sour Cream Pie

1	egg	1 cup	chopped raisins, dates OR
1 cup	sugar		currants OR ¼ cup
¼ tsp.	salt		chopped nuts and ¾ cup
½ tsp.	ground cloves OR allspice		chopped diced fruit
1 tsp.	cinnamon		
⅔ cup	thick sour cream OR buttermilk		

Beat egg only enough to blend, add sugar, salt and spice. Stir in sour cream and raisins. Pour into pastry-lined pie plate.

Bake in 450°F oven for 10 minutes, then lower oven to 350°F for 20-25 minutes or until filling is firm.

We like this pie with a mixture of raisins and chopped nuts, and fresh cow's cream gives a much better flavour than store-bought cream.

Thos. N. Musgrove, M.L.A.
Bow Valley
Alberta

Pumpkin Pie

½ cup	brown sugar	1½ cups	mashed pumpkin
½ cup	white sugar	2	eggs, well beaten
½ tsp.	salt	1 cup	light cream
1 tsp.	ginger	2 tsp.	tapioca
1 tsp.	cinnamon	1	unbaked pie shell
¼ tsp.	cloves		

Beat all together. Pour into unbaked pie shell. Bake at 425°F for 15 minutes, then at 350°F for 30 minutes.

Geoff and Eileen Wilson
Geoff Wilson, M.P.
Swift Current - Maple Creek
Saskatchewan

Butterscotch Pie

1 cup	milk	pinch	salt
2 tbsp.	butter (not margarine)	2	egg yolks, beaten
1 cup	brown sugar	1 tsp.	vanilla
5 tbsp.	flour	1	baked pie shell
3 tbsp.	cold milk		

Meringue:

2	egg whites	1 tsp.	cream of tartar
2 tbsp.	white sugar		

Scald milk and butter in double boiler or on top of stove. In a separate bowl, in order given, combine the sugar, flour and milk. Stir until creamy and add a pinch of salt. Add this to milk on stove and bring to a boil, stirring or whisking constantly to prevent sticking. When thickened stir a small amount into egg yolks, slowly stir egg yolks into rest of hot mixture and bring to boil again, stirring constantly. Remove from stove, stir in vanilla and set aside to cool, about 10 minutes, stirring occasionally.

To make meringue, beat egg whites very stiff, add sugar and cream of tartar.

Pour pie filling into cooked pie shell, top with meringue and brown under boiler.

Clarence and Bernette Cormier
Hon. Clarence Cormier, M.L.A.
Memramcook
New Brunswick

Impossible Pie

4	eggs	1 cup	white sugar
¼ cup	margarine	1 cup	coconut
½ cup	flour	2 tsp.	vanilla
2 cups	milk		

Blend all ingredients in blender for a few seconds until well mixed. Pour mixture into a deep 10" greased pie plate. Bake at 350°F for approximately 1 hour until centre tests firm.

The flour will settle to form a crust; the coconut forms the topping and the centre is an egg custard filling. This is very good on its own and is delicious with whipped cream.

Hon. Jerry Lawrence, M.L.A.
Halifax St. Margaret's
Nova Scotia

Lemon Sponge

This is a recipe that my Danish mother and grandmother have made for as long as I can remember.

4	eggs	1	lemon, juice and grated rind
¾ cup	sugar	½-1 cup	whipping cream, whipped
1	pkg. unflavoured gelatin		
½ cup	cold water		

Beat egg yolks with sugar until almost white. Dissolve gelatin in cold water. Heat until dissolved. Add to egg yolk mixture juice of 1 lemon and grated rind of ½ lemon. Add gelatin when slightly cooled. Fold in whipped cream and the stiffly-beaten egg whites. Cool for several hours and garnish.

Hon. Ray Hnatyshyn, P.C., M.P.
Saskatoon West
Saskatchewan

Cream Puffs

Choux Mixture:

1¼ cups	water	1 oz.	Oetker Gustin (cornstarch)
2 oz.	butter, margarine or lard	5-7	eggs
6 oz.	plain flour	1 tsp.	tsp. Oetker Backin (baking powder)

For the choux mixture, put the water and the fat into a pan, preferably with a long handle, bring to a boil and remove from heat. Stir in the flour, mixed and sieved with the Gustin (cornstarch) and stir until a smooth lump is formed. Heat the lump for about a minute, stirring constantly. Transfer the hot lump to a bowl and beat in the eggs one by one. When the mixture is a very glossy and of a good dropping consistency, no more eggs need be added. Cool slightly, then add the Backin (baking powder). With 2 spoons or a forcing bag, form the mixture into walnut-sized balls and place on a greased and slightly floured baking sheet.

Bake on low rack in 400°F oven for 5 minutes, reduce to 350°F and bake 25-30 minutes longer, or until quite firm to the touch. Do not open the oven door for the first 20 minutes' baking time, or the puffs will collapse. Cut them open immediately when they are done to allow steam to escape.

Filling:

3 tbsp.	Bird's custard powder	2 cups	hot milk
3 tbsp.	sugar		icing sugar
5 tbsp.	milk	2 cups	whipping cream

For the filling, stir the pudding powder and the sugar together and combine with the 5 tbsp. of milk. Bring the ¾ pint of milk to the boil, remove from heat, stir in the pudding powder mixture. Bring to the boil again, stirring all the time. Set aside to cool, stirring fairly often to avoid the formation of skin. Add a little icing sugar to the cream and whip until stiff. Fold into pudding.

Fill cream puffs.

Frank Oberle, M.P.
Prince George-Peace River
British Columbia

Poires avec Camembert

4	ripe but firm pears		strawberries, fresh OR
	Camembert cheese		thawed
	ginger	4	bay leaves

Core the pears from the bottom, leaving the top intact. Fill cavity with Camembert cheese. Place each in an individual baking dish and sprinkle with powdered ginger. Spoon strawberries and strawberry juice over each and insert a bay leaf in the top of each pear. Bake in a warm oven 10-15 minutes to warm pear and melt cheese. Serve immediately.

Norman Warner, M.P.
Stormont-Dundas
Ontario

No-Bake Mincemeat Mallow Cheesecake

1 cup	vanilla OR graham crumbs	2 x 8 oz.	pkgs. Philadelphia cream
¼ cup	margarine OR butter, melted		cheese, softened (250 g
1¾ cup	mincemeat		each)
4 cups	miniature marshmallows	2 tsp.	grated orange rind
⅓ cup	orange juice	1 cup	heavy cream, whipped
	Grand Marnier, optional		

Combine crumbs and margarine, press onto bottom of 9" springform pan. Chill.
Spread mincemeat over crust. Melt marshmallows with orange juice and a shot of Grand Marnier in double boiler, stir until smooth. Chill until thickened. Combine softened cream cheese with orange rind, beating until well blended and fluffy. Whip in marshmallow mixture. Fold in whipped cream. Pour over mincemeat. Chill until firm. Garnish with Mandarin orange sections and mint leaves. 10-12 servings.

Hon. James Snow, M.P.P.
Oakville
Ontario

Cheesecake

This is by far the best cheesecake I have ever eaten. It is courtesy of the very capable staff at the Henwood Institute who developed it for the 1984 Awards Dinner of the Alberta Alcohol and Drug Abuse Commission.

Crust:

1½ cups	finely ground vanilla wafer crumbs	2 tbsp.	brown sugar
		4 tbsp.	butter, melted
¾ cup	finely ground hazelnuts, pecans OR almonds		

Filling:

24 oz.	cream cheese (750 g)	4	eggs
1 cup	white sugar	1 tsp.	vanilla

Topping:

2 cups	sour cream		additional nuts, toasted, for garnish
3 tbsp.	sugar		
1 tsp.	vanilla		fresh fruit for garnish

In bowl, combine crumbs, nuts, sugar and butter. Pat the mixture onto the bottom and sides of an 8" springform pan or divide between 2, 8" pie plates if you prefer. (The smaller sizes are great for tucking away in the freezer.) Refrigerate.

Heat oven to 350°F. In a mixing bowl, cream the cheese and gradually beat in the sugar. Add eggs and vanilla and blend until smooth. Pour into crust and bake until set — about 45 minutes. Do not overcook; the filling should just be firm. Set aside to cool while you make the topping. Combine sour cream, sugar and vanilla and spread evenly over cheesecake. Bake for another 5 minutes. Cool, then refrigerate or freeze. This can be made a day or two ahead. Garnish with fresh strawberries and kiwi fruit or with sliced peaches.

John Gogo, M.L.A.
Lethbridge West
Alberta

Mousse Au Café

32	marshmallows	2 cups	whipping cream
¾ cup	of coffee		cherries and/or nuts

Cook marshmallows in coffee over medium heat until melted. Cool. Beat cream until stiff, then mix with marshmallow-coffee mixture. Decorate with cherries or nuts.

Jacques and Renée Flynn
Hon. Jacques Flynn
The Senate
Québec

Blueberry Cream Dessert

1¼ cups	crushed graham crackers	1 cup	dairy sour cream
¼ cup	sugar	8 oz.	carton blueberry yogurt
⅓ cup	butter OR margarine, melted	½ tsp.	vanilla
½ cup	sugar	½ cup	whipping cream, whipped
1	envelope unflavoured gelatin	1 cup	fresh OR frozen blueberries

In a bowl combine graham crackers, the ¼ cup sugar, and melted butter or margarine. Reserve ¼ cup crumb mixture; press remaining mixture into bottom of 10" x 6" x 2" dish. In a saucepan combine the ½ cup sugar and gelatin; add ¾ cup water. Heat and stir until gelatin and sugar dissolve. Combine sour cream and yogurt; gradually blend in gelatin mixture. Add vanilla. Chill until partially set. Fold into whipped cream. Stir in blueberries. Turn into the crust. Sprinkle reserved crumbs on top. Chill until set. Makes 8 servings.

Bruce Halliday, M.D., M.P.
Oxford
Ontario

Apple Bavarian Torte

½ cup	margarine OR butter		1	egg
⅓ cup	sugar		½ tsp.	vanilla
¼ tsp.	vanilla		⅓ cup	sugar
1 cup	flour		½ tsp.	cinnamon
8 oz.	pkg. Philadelphia cream cheese		4 cups	sliced, peeled apples
			¼ cup	sliced almonds
¼ cup	sugar			whipped cream

Cream butter, sugar, and vanilla. Blend in flour. Spread dough on bottom and sides of 9" springform pan. Combine softened cream cheese and sugar, add egg and vanilla, mix well. Pour into pastry-lined pan. Combine sugar and cinnamon. Toss apples in sugar mixture. Spoon mixture over cream cheese layer. Sprinkle with almonds. Bake at 425°F 10 minutes. Reduce to 375°F, continue baking 25 minutes. Loosen torte from rim of pan. Cool before removing rim of pan. Serve with a ring of whipped cream.

Hon. Julian Koziak, Q.C., M.L.A.
Edmonton Strathcona
Alberta

Rhubarb Torte

Base:

1 cup	flour		2 tbsp.	white sugar
¼ tsp.	salt		½ cup	soft butter

Topping:

1¼ cups	white sugar		½ cup	cream or evaporated milk
2 tbsp.	flour		2¼ cups	rhubarb in 1" pieces
3	egg yolks			

Meringue:

3	egg whites		¼ cup	white sugar

Crumble first 4 ingredients and press into 8" x 8" pan. Bake at 325°F for 25 minutes. Combine ingredients for topping and cook until thick and clear. Cool. Pour over base. Beat egg white and cover with meringue. Brown at 425°F for 5-10 minutes. Serves 9.

Hon. Marion Reid, M.L.A.
First Queens
Prince Edward Island

P.M.'s Dessert

| 14 | chocolate wafers | 1¼ cups | miniature marshmallows |
| 1 cup | whipping cream | ½ cup | crushed peppermint candy |

Crush chocolate wafers until fine. Using half of the crumbs cover bottom of a 9" x 9" pan evenly. Whip cream, fold in marshmallows and peppermint candy, carefully spoon onto crumbs. Sprinkle remaining crumbs on top, and refrigerate for at least 12 hours.

Peter M. Pope, M.L.A.
Fifth Prince
Prince Edward Island

Graham Wafer Pineapple Squares

This dessert is a definite favourite from coast to coast. As a variation, the Jepson's recipe combines ¾ cup of brown sugar with 2 cups of crumbs and the butter for the crust.

2½ cups	graham wafers, crushed	14 oz.	can crushed pineapple
1 cup	butter (½ cup melted)	1 cup	whipping cream, whipped
1½ cups	icing sugar	½ cup	sugar (to whip cream)
2	eggs		

Mix 2¼ cups crumbs with the ½ cup melted butter. Press into 8" x 8" pan and bake 15 minutes at 325°F oven. Let cool.

Cream ½ cup butter, gradually blending in icing sugar. Add eggs, beat until very light. Spread evenly over first mixture. Drain can of pineapple and fold into the whipped cream. Spread over mixture. Top with ¼ cup graham wafer crumbs. Set in refrigerator to chill.

Jim Gordon, M.L.A.
Miramichi Bay
New Brunswick
and
Robert L. Wenman, M.P.
Fraser Valley West
British Columbia

and
Jim and Bev Jepson
Jim Jepson, M.P.
London East
Ontario

Kiksekage

¾ cup	sugar	1 cup	cocoa
3	egg whites	1 tsp.	vanilla
1 cup	butter		Social Tea biscuits

Beat sugar and egg whites until white and foamy. Melt butter on stove, add cocoa and vanilla. Stir quickly and add to the beaten egg whites. Continue to beat. Line a loaf pan with wax paper. Pour 1 layer of chocolate. Then put 1 layer of Social Tea biscuits. Alternate chocolate and biscuits until all the chocolate is used. End with chocolate. Sprinkle with Trimits and refrigerate.

Stan Schellenberger, M.P.
Wetaskiwin
Alberta

Toasted Snow Squares

1 tbsp.	gelatin	3	egg whites, unbeaten
4 tbsp.	cold water	pinch	salt
1 cup	boiling water	1 tsp.	vanilla
⅔ cup	white sugar		

Sprinkle gelatin over cold water and let soak 5 minutes. Add boiling water and stir until dissolved. Add sugar gradually and let cool until it begins to stiffen, then add egg whites, salt and vanilla. Beat with egg beater until light. Pour into a greased 12" x 8" pan. Cut in squares when set and roll in graham wafer crumbs. Serve with sauce below.

Sauce:

3	egg yolks	bit	of melted butter
¼-½ cup	water	1 tbsp.	grated lemon rind, optional
⅓ cup	sugar		juice of ½ lemon

Stir water into yolks. Stir in sugar, then rest of ingredients. Cook in double boiler until thick. Stir constantly.

Doug and Audry Gourlay
Doug Gourlay, M.L.A.
Swan River
Manitoba

Ice Cream Squares

70	Ritz crackers, crushed	1½ cups	milk
¾ cup	melted margarine	2 qts.	vanilla ice cream
2 x 4 oz.	vanilla instant pudding		Dream Whip, prepared

Combine crumbs with margarine. Set aside ½ cup and press rest into 9" x 9" pan. Combine pudding mix with milk. Gradually beat in the ice cream. Pour this over crumb base. Spread with the Dream Whip and sprinkle on rest of crumbs. Freeze.

Hon. Leland W. McGaw, M.L.A.
Charlotte West
New Brunswick

Grapefruit Surprise Squares

2 x 1 lb.	cans grapefruit sections	2 tbsp.	milk
2 x 3 oz.	pkg. lemon Jell-o (85 g each)	½ cup	chopped walnuts, optional
8 oz.	pkg. cream cheese, at room temp.		maraschino cherries, optional

Drain grapefruit and add enough water to the syrup to make 3½ cups. Heat half the syrup mixture to boiling, add to Jell-o and stir until dissolved. Add remaining syrup mixture; cool. Reserve best grapefruit sections, about half, for top layer, arrange remaining in bottom of 9" x 9" pan. Carefully pour half the Jell-o over grapefruit in pan, chill until firm.

Soften cream cheese, add milk and nuts. Spread over Jell-o layer working from outside in. Chill. Meanwhile chill remaining Jell-o until partially set. Arrange reserved grapefruit on top of cheese, garnish with cherries, if desired, and carefully pour remaining Jell-o over top. Chill until set.

Cut in squares and serve on greens. 9-12 servings. Recipe can be halved and made in jelly mould. Very nice with ham or chicken or as a light luncheon dessert.

Alan and Louise Redway
Alan Redway, M.P.
York East
Ontario

Raspberry Delight

1¼ cups	graham crumbs		1 cup	boiling water
¼ cup	white sugar		15 oz.	pkg. frozen raspberries
¼ cup	melted butter			(425 g)
½ tsp.	cinnamon		20	marshmallows
3 oz.	pkg. raspberry Jell-o (85 g)		½ cup	milk
			1 cup	whipped cream

Combine first 4 ingredients. Reserve ¼ cup for topping, press remainder in 8" x 8" pan. Disolve Jell-o in boiling water. Add frozen raspberries. Break up as they thaw. When partially set, pour over crust. Melt marshmallows in double boiler with milk. Fold in whipped cream. Spread over raspberry filling. Sprinkle with remaining ¼ cup of crumb mixture. Refrigerate overnight.

Pauline Browes, M.P.
Scarborough Centre
Ontario

Raspberry Treat

1 cup	graham wafer crumbs		1 tbsp.	lemon juice
2 tbsp.	butter		15 oz.	box frozen raspberries (425 g)
3 oz.	pkg. raspberry Jell-o (85 g)			
1 cup	boiling water		½ cup	icing sugar
4 oz.	(25 g) pkg. Philadelphia		1 tsp.	vanilla
pinch	cream cheese		2 cups	whipping cream
	salt			

Combine crumbs and butter and pack into 8" x 8" greased pan. Dissolve Jell-o in boiling water, stir in lemon juice and raspberries, and chill until wobbly, 10-15 minutes. Cream together the cream cheese, salt, icing sugar and vanilla. Whip cream until stiff and fold into cheese mixture. Put Jell-o layer, then cream cheese layer onto base. Chill.

Garry Filmon, M.L.A.
Leader of the Opposition
Tuxedo
Manitoba

Scotch Trifle

This dessert is excellent for large groups and can be prepared well in advance and kept refrigerated.

1	raspberry Swiss roll	3 oz.	pkg. strawberry Jell-o (85 g)
19 oz.	can fruit cocktail	5 oz.	pkg. vanilla pudding (135 g)
1 tbsp.	Harveys' Bristol Cream sherry		whipped cream

Slice Swiss roll and arrange in deep glass bowl. Drain fruit cocktail and scatter over top. Drizzle on sherry. Prepare Jell-o according to package directions and pour over fruit. Allow to set. Prepare pudding according to package directions, cool slightly and pour over Jell-o. Spread whipped cream decoratively on top when pudding has cooled.

Many variations are possible on this theme. e.g. lemon cake, mandarin orange segments, lemon jelly, or chocolate as the flavouring.

Hon. Colin Maxwell, M.L.A.
Turtleford
Saskatchewan

English Trifle (Polish Version)

9-10 oz.	pkg. white or yellow cake mix (278 g)	15 oz.	box frozen sweetened strawberries, defrosted
19 oz.	can fruit cocktail	3 oz.	box Jell-o (85 g)
	vodka		Bird's custard powder
	sweet liqueur (Grand Marnier, Cointreau, etc.)	1 cup	whipping cream
			fresh fruit for topping

Make cake mix according to instructions on package. Marinate drained fruit cocktail in vodka for 2 hours. Break cake into small pieces and spread on bottom of a large glass bowl. Sprinkle with liqueur; do not soak too much.

Drain fruit cocktail and strawberries. Spread evenly over cake. Make Jell-o. When almost set, pour over cake and fruit.

Make 1½ or double the amount of custard in recipe on Bird's can. When cooked and partially set, pour over previous layers. Whip cream, adding sugar to taste. Spread evenly over custard. Top with kiwi slices or other fresh fruit.

Walter Szwender, M.L.A.
Edmonton Belmont
Alberta

Mandarin Tipsy Trifle

	custard (recipe follows)	2 x 10 oz.	cans mandarin orange
1	small pound cake or Génoise		sections, drained
	or sponge cake	2 cups	whipping cream, whipped
¼ cup	orange liqueur OR orange		and sweetened
	juice		toasted almonds
			kiwi slices optional

Make and chill custard first. Cut cake into slices about ½"thick. Arrange half the slices in bottom of glass bowl. Sprinkle with half the liqueur or orange juice. Cover with half the custard, then half the mandarin sections, then half the whipped cream. Cover with remaining cake slices; sprinkle with remaining liqueur or juice and cover with remaining custard. Finish with layer of whipped cream. Arrange remaining mandarin sections, toasted almonds and kiwi slices (if used) on top. Chill for several hours before serving.

Makes about 10 servings.

Custard:

4	egg yolks	1 tbsp.	orange liqueur
¼ cup	granulated sugar		OR
2 cups	light cream, heated almost to	1 tsp.	vanilla
	boiling		

Beat egg yolks with sugar until thick. Stir in heated cream. Pour mixture into heavy saucepan or top of double boiler and cook over low heat or simmering water, stirring almost constantly until custard coats metal spoon. Remove from heat; stir in liqueur, cover and chill. Use as directed above.

Susan and Arnold Malone
Arnold Malone, M.P.
Crowfoot
Alberta

Fruit Crunch

1 cup	flour	4 cups	cut up fruit
¾ cup	rolled oats	1 cup	sugar
1 cup	packed brown sugar	2 tbsp.	cornstarch
½ cup	melted butter	1 cup	water
1 tsp.	cinnamon	1 tsp.	vanilla

Mix first 5 ingredients until crumbly. Press half the crumbs into a greased 9" baking pan. Cover with 4 cups of cut up fruit — rhubarb is especially good. Cook the last 4 ingredients until thick and clear and pour over the fruit. Top with the remaining crumbs.

Bake at 350°F for 1 hour or until it is golden. Cut into squares and serve warm — plain or with whipped cream.

Joe Clark, Maureen McTeer and Catherine Clark
The Rt. Hon. Joe Clark, P.C., M.P.
Yellowhead
Alberta

Tory Blue(Berry) Grunt

Dumplings:

2 cups	flour	3 tsp.	baking powder
3 tbsp.	sugar	2 tbsp.	shortening
1 tsp.	salt	1 cup	milk

To make dumplings, sift together flour, salt and baking powder. Cut in shortening. Add sugar. Gradually add milk. Mix smooth. Drop by tablespoons into hot water. Cover tightly. Cook 10 to 12 minutes.

Blueberry Sauce:

2 cups	blueberries	½ tsp.	cinnamon
¾ cup	sugar	¼ tsp.	nutmeg

Combine all ingredients. Bring to boiling point, boil 5 minutes. Stir occasionally. Serve hot sauce over dumplings. Whipping cream or ice cream is optional. Sauce is featured on front cover photograph.

Hon. Bob Mitchell, M.P.P.
Carleton
Ontario

Rich Plum Pudding

"My grandmother came from London, England in 1910 to the Prairies of Canada. She found many changes to her lifestyle. However, once her own family was started she carried on the tradition of the Rich Plum Pudding for Christmas, a tradition my own mother continued and then passed the recipe to me." Laura Kilgour.

1 lb.	seeded raisins	2 cups	flour
1 lb.	currants	¾ lb.	shredded suet
1 lb.	sultana raisins	2 tsp.	mixed spice
½ lb.	mixed peel	½ tsp.	salt
2 oz.	chopped blanched almonds	1 lb.	brown sugar
2	small lemons	4	eggs
4 cups	packed bread crumbs	2 cups	milk

Clean fruit, cut peel fine and chop almonds. Grate rind of lemons and strain juice. Mix bread crumbs, flour, suet, spices, salt, sugar, almonds, peel and grated lemon rind. Stir in fruit and add lemon juice. Beat eggs, add to milk and stir well into other ingredients. Grease pudding basins well, (we use small pyrex bowls), dust with sugar. Cover pudding with several thicknesses of stiff waxed paper then pudding cloth (a piece of tightly woven cotton). Tie down tightly and strongly with string. Boil pudding for 8 hours in large pot of water, placing a piece of wood under the bowls and making sure water level is below the level of the rim of the bowl. When cooked, take bowl from water, remove cloth and paper and let stand 10 minutes. Turn pudding out of bowl and let stand until thoroughly cold. When pudding has lost its dampness, wrap in foil. Store in cool place.

When ready to use pudding, place back in the bowl, cover again with waxed paper and cloth and boil a further 2 hours. Cut steaming pudding into wedges and serve with hard sauce or ice cream.

David and Laura Kilgour
David Kilgour, M.P.
Edmonton Strathcona
Alberta

Raspberry Dumpling

	raspberries	½ cup	milk
1 cup	flour	1	egg, beaten
1 tsp.	large tsp. baking powder (heaping tsp.)	2 tbsp.	melted butter
¼ tsp.	salt		
½-¾ cups	white sugar		

Place bed of raspberries in glass, ovenproof dish, and cover with sugar to individual taste. To make batter, mix dry ingredients together. Add liquids, mixing until it is absorbed. Drop by spoonfuls over raspberry bed. Sprinkle with sugar. Bake at 350-375°F until dough is cooked.

Serve hot, with a scoop of homemade vanilla ice cream.

Steven Porter, M.L.A.
Carleton South
New Brunswick

Steamed Blueberry Pudding

This favourite recipe has been in my family for many years.

½ cup	butter	1½ cups	flour
1 cup	brown sugar	¼ tsp.	salt
2	eggs	2 tsp.	baking powder
1 tsp.	vanilla	1 cup	blueberries
½ cup	milk		

Cream butter and sugar. Add eggs, vanilla and milk. Sift together flour, salt and baking powder. Add to butter mixture, then add blueberries. Mix and pour into pudding mould. Steam for 1½ hours.

As featured on the front cover photograph, this pudding was topped with Blueberry Sauce page 170 and flamed with cognac.

W. George Cross, M.H.A.
Bonavista North
Newfoundland and Labrador

Dublin Fruit Cake

½ cup	candied cherries, halved	¼ tsp.	nutmeg
¾ cup	whole blanched almonds	1 cup	OR ½ lb. unsalted butter
1½ cups	seedless black raisins	1 cup	sugar
1½ cups	golden raisins	6	eggs
1½ cups	currants		grated rind of ½ lemon
¾ cup	diced mixed candied fruit OR peel	½ tsp.	vanilla extract
2 tbsp.	chopped peeled apple	¼ tsp.	almond extract
2⅔ cups	flour (approximately)	3 oz.	Irish whiskey
½ tsp.	baking powder		
¼ tsp.	cinnamon		

Wash cherries and let them dry uncovered overnight. Grind ½ almonds and shred or coarsely chop the remaining half. Wash and dry raisins and currants. Combine all fruits and nuts, and toss to mix thoroughly. Sift flour twice with baking powder and spices and set aside.

Cream butter with sugar until light and fluffy. Beat eggs with lemon rind, vanilla, and almond extract. Add gradually to the butter mixture, beating well between additions.

Sift flour in gradually, stirring with a metal spoon. Add fruits and ½ whiskey and beat until well blended. This should be baked in an unfluted 9" tube pan or in a 9" round cake pan that is about 3" deep. Butter the pan and line with buttered brown paper or several thicknesses of buttered wax paper.

Turn batter into pan. If you are not using a tube pan, make a hollow in the centre of the batter so it will rise evenly and be flat. Bake in preheated 300°F oven for about 4 hours. If cake begins to brown too rapidly, cover with a sheet of buttered brown paper.

Sprinkle with remaining whiskey as soon as you take the cake from the oven. Cool in pan for 1 hour. Invert onto rack. Remove paper and cool completely. When dry, spread with either Almond Paste Icing or Royal Icing. Store in airtight container.

Paul, Barbara, Donna, Colleen and Sharon Meagher
Paul Meagher, M.L.A.
Prince Albert
Saskatchewan

Light Fruit Cake

1½ lbs.	glazed cherries		1 lb.	sugar (2 cups)
1½ lbs.	white raisins		1 lb.	eggs (10 large or 12 medium)
1 lb.	mixed fruit			
1 lb.	butter		1 lb.	all-purpose flour (3 cups)

Wash fruit; cream together butter and sugar. Add eggs. Mix fruit in flour and gradually add to mixture; mix well.

Spoon into pans that have been greased, lined with brown paper and greased again. Bake at 275°F 2½ to 3 hours or until done.

Bud and Susan Bradley
T. A. Bradley, C.D., D.D.S., M.P.
Haldimand-Norfolk
Ontario

Lemon Loaf

¼ cup	sugar		1½ cups	all-purpose flour
1	lemon		1 tsp.	baking powder
½ cup	butter		½ tsp.	salt
1 cup	sugar		½ cup	milk
2	eggs			

Heat oven 350°F. Grease loaf pan about 10¼" x 3½" x 2½". Grate rind from lemon and set aside. Squeeze out juice. Combine ¼ cup sugar and lemon juice in warm place until needed; stir occasionally. Cream butter and sugar, beat until fluffy. Add eggs one at a time, beating well after each addition. Sift flour, baking powder and salt together and add to creamed mixture alternately with milk. Stir in 2 tsp. of the grated lemon rind. Spoon into prepared pan and bake 45 minutes or until toothpick stuck in centre comes out clean. Leave in pan on cake rack and pour warmed lemon juice mixture slowly over loaf while it is still hot. Cool in pan. When cool, turn out of pan and wrap in aluminum foil. Store a day or two to mellow. Slice as desired. This cake freezes very well, and is not as fattening as iced cakes!

Bill and Doreen Doody
Hon. Bill Doody
The Senate
Newfoundland and Labrador

Banana Cake

1 cup	sugar	1½ tsp.	baking soda, dissolved in milk
½ cup	butter		mashed bananas (3)
1	egg	1 cup	flour
2 tbsp.	sweet milk	1½ cups	baking powder
		½ tsp.	

Mix together and pour into 2 small layer pans, a loaf pan, or 9" x 11" pan. Bake at 350°F for 25-30 minutes for cakes, or 50-60 minutes for loaf, or until done.

Lorne and Rita Henderson
Lorne C. Henderson, M.P.P.
Lambton
Ontario

Spice Cup Cakes

1 cup	raisins	1 tsp.	baking soda
1½ cups	water	1½ cups	flour
½ cup	butter	1 tsp.	cloves
¾ cup	sugar	1 tsp.	cinnamon
1	egg		

Boil raisins in 1½ cups water for 10 minutes. Meanwhile, combine other ingredients, add raisins after they have cooled a bit.

Bake in 375°F oven for 20-25 minutes. Ice with your favourite white icing.

Albert and Mary Driedger
Albert Driedger, M.L.A.
Emerson
Manitoba

Caroline's Featherweight Cake

1 cup	sugar	pinch	salt
3	eggs	½ cup	milk
1 cup	flour		butter, size of egg
1½ tsp.	baking powder	1 tsp.	vanilla

Beat sugar and eggs until very light. Sift dry ingredients together and add to egg mixture. Heat milk and butter to boiling point, pour into batter and stir well. Add vanilla. Pour into greased and floured 8" x 8" pan and bake in 350°F oven 25-30 minutes, or until done. When cool ice with Boiled Icing.

Boiled Icing

¾ cup	white OR brown sugar	1	egg white
1½ tbsp.	water	1 tsp.	vanilla
1 tbsp.	corn syrup		

Mix ingredients, except vanilla, together, then place over medium heat and beat with portable beater (or hand beater) for 4-5 minutes, or until of spreading consistency. Add vanilla, beat a bit more if necessary. Spread on cake. Coconut, or chopped nuts may be sprinkled on top.

Bob and Beryl Elliott
Bob Elliott, M.L.A.
Grande Prairie
Alberta

Potato Pound Cake

1 cup	soft butter	½ cup	finely mashed P.E.I. potatoes
1 cup	sugar	1 tsp.	nutmeg (optional)
1 tsp.	grated lemon rind	½ tsp.	baking powder
1 tsp.	lemon juice	1¾ cups	presifted flour
4	eggs		

Grease and flour 9" x 5" x 3" loaf pan. Beat butter and sugar for 4 minutes. Mix in juice and rind. Beat in eggs 1 at a time, beat 1 minute after each egg. Beat until smooth, 5 minutes. Add potatoes, mix well. Mix together dry ingredients, and add gradually. Bake at 325°F for 1 hour. Beating is important for success. Best in 1 or 2 days.

Hon. George R. McMahon, Q.C., M.L.A.
Fifth Prince
Prince Edward Island

My Favourite Toasted Coconut Cake

2	eggs	1 tsp.	cinnamon
1 cup	sugar	½ cup	milk
1 cup	flour	¾ cup	walnuts
1 tsp.	baking powder		

Beat eggs until they are very light, then add sugar and continue beating until it is dissolved and mixture thickens. Measure flour before you sift it, then sift with baking powder and cinnamon. Add to egg mixture alternately with the milk. Batter should be very thin. Pour into a shallow pan lined with wax paper, sprinkle with nuts. Bake at 375°F for about 25 minutes until cake rises and begins to turn brown, remove from oven, spread topping over. Return to the oven for 10 or 15 minutes longer, until delicate brown.

Topping:

3 tbsp.	butter	2 tbsp.	cream
5 tbsp.	brown sugar	½ cup	coconut

Cream butter, sugar, cream; stir in coconut. Spread over the partially baked cake.

Walter and Dorathea Johnson
Walter Johnson, M.L.A.
Saltcoats
Saskatchewan

Raspberry Coffee Cake

3 oz.	cream cheese	⅓ cup	milk
¼ cup	butter	½ cup	raspberry preserves
2 cups	packaged biscuit mix		

Cut cream cheese and butter into biscuit mix until crumbly. Blend in milk. Turn out onto lightly floured surface and knead 8 to 10 strokes. On waxed paper, roll dough to 12" x 8" rectangle. Turn onto greased baking sheet; remove waxed paper. Spread raspberry preserves down centre of dough. Make 2½" cuts at intervals on long sides. Fold strips over filling. Bake at 425°F for 12 to 15 minutes. Drizzle the warm coffee cake with Confectioner's Icing (recipe follows). Makes 1 coffee cake.

Confectioner's Icing

1 cup	sifted icing sugar	1½ tbsp.	milk
¼ tsp.	vanilla		

Combine ingredients and drizzle over Raspberry Coffee Cake.

Hon. E. G. Allen
Fredericton North
New Brunswick

Sour Cream Cake

1 cup	white sugar	1 tsp.	cinnamon
2	eggs, at room temperature	1 tsp.	baking soda
6 tbsp.	margarine, softened	1 cup	sour cream
1½ cups	all-purpose flour	6 oz.	semisweet chocolate chips
1½ tsp.	baking powder		

Beat together sugar, eggs, and margarine for 10 minutes. Fold in flour, baking powder, cinnamon, and baking soda. Fold in sour cream. Place in 13" x 9" greased pan. Sprinkle with chocolate chips. Bake at 350°F for 30 to 35 minutes. Serve warm.

Hon. Allan K. McLean, M.P.P.
Simcoe East
Ontario

Applesauce Cake

2 cups	sugar	1 cup	chopped walnuts
1 cup	butter	2 cups	white raisins
3½ cups	sifted flour	2 tsp.	soda
1 tsp.	baking powder		hot water
2 tsp.	cinnamon	2 cups	unsweetened applesauce
1 tsp.	cloves	1½ tsp.	vanilla

Cream sugar and butter. Sift dry ingredients, except soda, add nuts and raisins. Dissolve soda in hot water, add to butter and sugar. Combine with dry ingredients. Add applesauce and mix well. Add vanilla. Bake in greased 9" x 13" pan at 350°F for about 1 hour.

Hon. Michael Wilson, P.C., M.P.
Etobicoke Centre
Ontario

Top Me-Twice Cake

Cake:

2 cups	all-purpose flour	13½ oz.	can OR 1½ cups crushed
1 cup	sugar		pineapple, not drained
1 tsp.	salt	1 tsp.	vanilla
1 tsp.	soda	2	eggs

Topping:

½ cup	firmly packed brown sugar	½ cup	flaked coconut
		½ cup	chopped pecans

Sauce:

½ cup	butter OR margarine	½ cup	sugar
½ cup	light cream	½ tsp.	vanilla

Heat oven to 350°F. 9" x 9" pan. Combine all cake ingredients in a large bowl. Blend on low until blended — then 2 minutes on medium. Pour into 9" pan, greased on bottom only. Sprinkle with topping. Bake 45-50 minutes, or until knife comes out clean. Top should spring back when touched. Just before cake is done, melt sauce ingredients, slowly, in a saucepan, pour over warm cake; cool before serving.

Perrin and Julie Beatty
Hon. Perrin Beatty, P.C., M.P.
Wellington-Dufferin-Simcoe
Ontario

Prune Cake

This cake is a longtime family favourite.

½ cup	shortening	1 tsp.	baking soda
1½ cups	brown sugar	1 tsp.	cinnamon
2	eggs, beaten	1 tsp.	cloves
2½ cups	flour	1 tsp.	allspice
1 tsp.	salt	1 cup	sour milk OR buttermilk
1 tsp.	baking powder	1 cup	cooked chopped prunes

Cream together shortening and sugar. Beat in the eggs. Sift flour and spices. Add alternately with sour milk. Add prunes. Pour into greased 9" x 12" pan. Bake in 350°F oven 40-45 minutes.

Allan and Elizabeth McKinnon
Hon. Allan McKinnon, P.C., M.P.
Victoria
British Columbia

Rhubarb Upside Down Cake

4 cups	fresh rhubarb	1 tsp.	vanilla
4 tsp.	melted butter	1½ cups	sifted cake flour
⅔ cup	brown sugar	½ tsp.	salt
¼ cup	shortening OR butter	2½ tsp.	baking powder
⅔ cup	sugar	¾ cup	milk
1	egg		

Wash rhubarb and cut in 1½" pieces. Mix butter and sugar and spread rhubarb, butter and sugar in 9" square pan.

Cream shortening, gradually add sugar and blend well. Add egg and beat mixture until light and creamy. Add vanilla.

Sift together dry ingredients. Add alternately with milk beating slightly after each addition. Pour over rhubarb mixture and bake in moderate oven at 350°F 45-50 minutes.

Serve with whipped cream or ice cream on top.

Jim Caldwell, M.P.
Essex-Kent
Ontario

Sultana Cake

2 cups	sultana raisins	2 cups	white sugar
½ lb.	mixed peel	4	eggs
½ lb.	cherries	2 tsp.	baking powder
3½ cups	flour	1 cup	milk
1 cup	butter	1 tsp.	lemon extract

Prepare raisins, peel and cherries by dredging with ½ cup of the flour. Set aside. Cream butter and sugar until light and fluffy. Add eggs one at a time and beat well. Sift flour and baking powder together. Add flour alternately with milk to the batter. Add lemon extract and fold in the prepared fruit. Pour in pans: 2, 9" x 9" or 1, 9" x 13". Bake in 350°F oven for about 1 hour.

Hon. Joe Mombourquette, M.L.A.
Oromocto
New Brunswick

Carrot Nut Cake or Loaf

2 cups	sifted all-purpose flour	1 cup	vegetable oil
2 tsp.	baking powder	4	eggs
1 tsp.	baking soda	3 cups	grated raw carrots
1 tsp.	salt	1 cup	finely chopped walnuts
2 tsp.	cinnamon		candied cherries, halved,
2 cups	sugar		optional

Preheat oven 325°F. Oil and line bottom of 2, 9" x 5" loaf pans or 2, 9" round layer pans with wax paper. Sift together flour, baking powder, baking soda, salt and cinnamon.

Add sugar gradually to oil, beating well after each addition with electric mixer at high speed. Beat egg until very light. Gradually beat them a little at a time, into oil-sugar mixture. Continue beating until mixture is smooth and fluffy.

Gradually stir in sifted dry ingredients until thoroughly combined. Add carrots, nuts and cherries if used, and mix well. Pour into pans and bake about 1½ hours.

Allow to cool about 20 minutes before removing from pans.

M. C. Rybchuk, M.L.A.
Regina Victoria
Saskatchewan

Frosted Carrot Cake

This delicious cake is the favourite of two Maritime families.

2½ cups	all-purpose flour		1 tsp.	baking soda
2 cups	sugar		½ tsp.	salt
1¼ cups	salad oil		4	eggs
⅓ cup	milk		3 cups	extra-finely grated
2 tsp.	baking powder			carrots
2 tsp.	cinnamon		1 cup	chopped walnuts

Preheat oven to 325°F. Grease 10" tube pan. Into large bowl, measure first 9 ingredients until just mixed. Increase speed to high and beat 5 minutes, occasionally scraping bowl with rubber spatula. Stir in carrots and nuts. Pour batter into pan. Bake 1 hour and 15 minutes or until toothpick inserted in centre comes out clean. Cool cake in pan on wire rack for 10 minutes. Remove from pan and cool completely. Frost with Fluffy Cream Cheese Frosting.

Fluffy Cream Cheese Frosting

4 oz.	pkg. cream cheese		3½-4 cups	icing sugar
½ cup	margarine		¼ cup	chopped nuts
1 tsp.	vanilla			

Beat together. If necessary add a little milk to bring to spreading consistency.

Hon. Paul Dawson, M.L.A.
Miramichi - Newcastle
New Brunswick
and
John Butt, M.H.A.
Conception Bay South
Newfoundland and Labrador

Carrot Cake

¾ cup	Mazola corn oil	1⅓ tsp.	baking soda
1 cup	sugar	1½ tsp.	cinnamon
3	eggs	2 cups	finely grated carrots
1½ cups	flour	½ cup	walnuts
½ tsp.	salt		

Beat oil and sugar together until fluffy. Add eggs one at a time and beat well after each. Sift dry ingredients and add to creamed mixture. Beat until well blended. Fold in raw carrots and chopped nuts.

Bake 1 hour at 300°F in greased 9" x 13"pan.

Icing For Carrot Cake:

8 oz.	Philadelphia cream cheese	2½ cups	icing sugar
4 tbsp.	butter (do not substitute)	2 tsp.	vanilla

Soften cheese and butter and beat well. Add sugar and vanilla. Beat again. Spread on cooled cake.

Ron Moore, M.L.A.
Lacombe
Alberta

Eggnog Cake

1	angel food cake	½ cup	rum
½ lb.	(1 cup) butter	¼ cup	toasted sliced almonds
1 lb.	icing sugar	2 cups	whipping cream, whipped
5	egg yolks	2 tbsp.	rum

Split angel food cake into three layers. Cream butter and icing sugar. Blend in egg yolks, ½ cup of rum, and almonds, and spread between layers. Beat together cream, sugar and the 2 tbsp. rum. Spread on top of cake. Serves 12 or more.

Keith Dow, M.L.A.
Saint John West
New Brunswick

Gumdrop Cake

½ lb.	butter OR 1 cup shortening, instead, for a nice moist cake	1 tsp.	baking powder
		½ tsp.	salt
		½ tsp.	vanilla
2 cups	white sugar	1 tsp.	almond extract
3	eggs	½ tsp.	lemon juice
3 cups	flour (set aside 1 cup to flour the gumdrops)	1 cup	milk
		2 lbs.	gumdrops*

Cream butter and sugar together well. Make sure they are very well mixed. Mix in remaining ingredients, pour into greased bundt or tube pan and bake for 2 hours at 300-325°F. Cook the cake until the top is just a light beige colour. If you find the top is getting too dark, place a piece of waxed paper over it.

*Orange and yellow "half-moon" gumdrops work the best since they are more moist.

Mel and Lois Gass
Mel Gass, M.P.
Malpeque
Prince Edward Island

Poppy Seed Chiffon Cake

2 cups	flour	½ cup	vegetable oil
1½ cups	white sugar	7	eggs, separated
3 tsp.	baking powder	2 tsp.	vanilla
1 tsp.	salt	¼ tsp.	baking soda
½ cup	poppy seeds	½ tsp.	cream of tartar
1 cup	water		

Combine first 5 ingredients. Make a well in the middle and add the remaining ingredients except egg whites and cream of tartar. Beat mixture until smooth. In a separate bowl, beat egg whites with cream of tartar until very stiff. Pour egg whites into poppy seed mixture and gently fold in. Pour into ungreased tube pan and bake for 55 minutes at 325°F. This is a very high cake.

Ben, Lucie, Suzanne, Clarence, Lori-Anne, Jennifer Boutin
Ben Boutin, M.L.A.
Kinistino
Saskatchewan

Unbaked Chocolate Cake

½ cup	butter	1 tsp.	vanilla
1 cup	white sugar	¾ cup	chopped walnuts
2 tbsp.	cocoa, heaping	1 cup	graham wafer crumbs
1	beaten egg		

Melt butter in pan, add sugar, cocoa and egg. Stir. Bring to a boil and simmer 1 minute. Add vanilla, nuts and crumbs. Press mixture into greased 9" x 9" pan and ice with chocolate icing. Sprinkle with nuts. Don't bake.

Icing:

1 tbsp.	butter		vanilla OR peppermint
2 tbsp.	cocoa		icing sugar
2 tbsp.	milk		

Melt butter and cocoa together and add milk. Flavour with vanilla or peppermint. Add enough icing sugar to make spreadable.

Lee and Barbara Clark
Lee Clark, M.P.
Brandon - Souris
Manitoba

Fudge Brownies

½ cup	margarine	1 cup	all-purpose flour
1 cup	white sugar	½ cup	cocoa
1 tsp.	vanilla	½ cup	chopped walnuts
2	eggs		

Mix well first 4 ingredients, stir in remaining ones and pour into 8" x 8" greased pan. Bake at 325°F for 25 minutes. When cool, ice with chocolate icing.

Duane Weiman, M.L.A.
Saskatoon - Fairview
Saskatchewan

Brownie Cake

This family recipe, is very popular with both family and friends. It makes a large cake and only takes 5 minutes to get into the oven.

¼ lb.	butter		2 tbsp.	vinegar
1 lb.	flour		1½ cups	cups milk
6 oz.	brown sugar		1½ tsp.	baking soda
½-1 lb.	raisins			

Rub butter into flour. Mix in sugar and fruit. Add vinegar to about 1½ cups of milk. Add soda to milk. Stir. Add to ingredients and mix, adding more milk if necessary to make a sticky batter.

Bake 2-3 hours at about 225°F — very slowly — in a large, 9" x 13", greased and floured baking tin.

Pat and Pat Crofton
Patrick D. Crofton, M.P.
Esquimalt - Saanich
British Columbia

Chocolate Sundae Pudding

1 cup	flour		1 tsp.	vanilla
2 tsp.	baking powder		½ cup	brown sugar
1 tsp.	salt		¼ cup	white sugar
2 tbsp.	cocoa		3 tbsp.	cocoa
⅔ cup	sugar		1 tsp.	vanilla
½ cup	milk		¼ tsp.	salt
2 tbsp.	melted butter OR margarine		1 cup	boiling water

Sift first 5 ingredients together in mixing bowl. Add milk, melted butter and vanilla, and mix well. Pour into greased 1-quart casserole. Mix together sugar, cocoa, vanilla and salt. Spread this mixture evenly over batter. Pour 1 cup boiling water over all. Do not stir. Bake in moderate oven at 350°F for 1 hour. Cover casserole during last ½ hour.

Robert and Mary Coates
Hon. Robert C. Coates, P.C., M.P.
Cumberland-Colchester
Nova Scotia

Cookie Sheet Chocolate Cake

2 cups	sugar	1 tsp.	baking soda
2 cups	flour	½ cup	buttermilk
pinch	salt	1 tsp.	vanilla
½ cup	oil	2	eggs, beaten
4 tbsp.	cocoa	1 cup	cold water
½ cup	margarine		

Mix first 3 ingredients. Boil oil, cocoa and margarine together and pour over flour mixture and stir. Dissolve baking soda in buttermilk and add. Mix vanilla in beaten eggs and add to above. Lastly, add cold water. Mix thoroughly. Pour into greased cookie sheet with sides. Bake at 400°F for 19 minutes. Ice while hot. This cake freezes very well.

Icing:

| ¼ cup | margarine | 2 tbsp. | milk |
| 2 tbsp. | cocoa | ½ cup | icing sugar |

Melt ingredients together and pour over the cake as soon as it comes out of the oven.

Harold Martens, M.L.A.
Morse
Saskatchewan

Miracle Whip Chocolate Cake

2 cups	sifted flour	¼ tsp.	salt
1 cup	white sugar	1 cup	hot water
1 tsp.	baking soda	2 tsp.	vanilla
1 tsp.	baking powder	1 cup	Miracle Whip
3 tbsp.	cocoa		

Mix together as listed. Bake in 8" square pan at 350°F for 35 minutes. Keeps well and can be frozen.

Bill Vankoughnet, M.P.
Hastings-Frontenac-Lennox & Addington
Ontario

Black Forest Cake

1 cup	sifted cake flour		3 cups	whipping cream
½ tsp.	baking powder		¼ cup	icing sugar
2 tbsp.	unsweetened cocoa		1 tbsp.	Kirsch
¼ tsp.	baking soda		19 oz.	can cherry pie filling — using mostly cherries and a little of the sauce
⅛ tsp.	salt			
2	eggs, separated, at room temp.		2 x 1 oz.	squares unsweetened chocolate
¼ cup	veg. shortening or oil			
⅔ cup	+ 2 tbsp. sugar (keeping separate)		12	maraschino cherries, with stems if possible
½ cup	buttermilk			

Grease and flour 3, 9" layer pans. Sift flour, baking powder, cocoa, baking soda and salt. In a large bowl, at high speed beat egg yolks, add shortening and ⅔ cup sugar and beat until smooth and fluffy. Turn to low speed and beat in buttermilk. Add flour mixture, beating just until blended — Don't overbeat. Beat egg whites in small bowl until foamy white. Gradually beat in remaining 2 tbsp. sugar until meringue forms soft peaks. Fold into cake batter. Divide batter among 3 pans, 1 cup in each. Bake 15 minutes at 350°F until centre springs back when lightly pressed. Cool on wire racks for 10 minutes. Loosen edges with knife, turn into racks and cool completely. Beat cream and icing sugar until stiff. Fold In Kirsch. Place 1 cake layer on plate. Spread cream on thickly, then a layer of pie filling. Use mostly cherries and a little of the sauce. Add second layer of cream. Top with second cake. On second cake spread about ¼ of whipping cream and pie filling. Add top layer, frost with cream on top and sides of cake. Decorate with rosettes of cream. Shave chocolate square with vegetable peeler. Press some chocolate curls along bottom of cake and remainder in centre of cake. Garnish with rosettes of cream with maraschino cherries and refrigerate. Serves 12.

Herb and Anita Swan
Hon. H. L. Swan, M.L.A.
Speaker
Rosetown - Elrose
Saskatchewan

Vinareterta

This Icelandic dish is a family tradition and comes from my mother-in-law.

1 cup	butter	1 tsp.	baking powder
1½ cups	sugar	¼ tsp.	ground cardamom
2	eggs	1 tsp.	vanilla
4 cups	flour	3 tbsp.	cream

Cream butter, add sugar, then eggs one at a time beating hard. Sift flour with baking powder and cardamom. Add a little of the sifted flour mixture. Add vanilla and cream, then work in as much flour as possible.

Knead in remaining flour. Divide dough into 5 or 6 equal parts and pat into 9" greased layer pans. Bake in 375°F oven until a delicate brown. Put together with prune filling, below. Allow to mellow at least 1 day.

Prune Filling:

1 lb.	prunes	½ cup	prune juice
½ cup	sugar	1 tbsp.	vanilla
1 tbsp.	cinnamon		

Cook prunes in water. When softened, remove, pit and purée in blender. Add sugar, cinnamon, and ½ cup of juice in which prunes were cooked. Cook together, add vanilla and cool. Spread between cake layers.

Charlotte L. Oleson, M.L.A.
Gladstone
Manitoba

Gord Walker's Butterscotch Squares

¾ cup	butter	3 cups	quick-cooking rolled oats
1 cup	dark brown sugar	⅛ tsp.	salt

Melt butter. Mix other 3 ingredients and add to butter. Press into 8" x 8" pan and cook at 350°F for 15 minutes. Cut when warm; let cool before taking out.

Hon. Gord Walker, Q.C., M.P.P.
London South
Ontario

Pineapple Cherry Squares

Base:

2 cups	sifted all-purpose flour	1 cup	margarine OR butter
2 tbsp.	sugar	1	egg yolk, well beaten

Filling:

15 oz.	can crushed pineapple	¼ cup	cold water
¼ cup	granulated sugar	½ cup	chopped maraschino cherries
2 tbsp.	cornstarch		

Topping:

2	egg whites	¼ tsp.	almond flavouring
2 tbsp.	sugar	½ cup	finely shredded coconut

Blend flour and sugar, rub in margarine until crumbly. Add beaten egg yolk to moisten slightly. Pat into 9" x 12" pan. Bake in a moderate oven for 20 minutes or until lightly browned. Bring pineapple and sugar to a slow boil. Mix cornstarch with cold water, add to boiling mixture, stir until thickened. Add chopped cherries. Spread evenly on base. Beat egg white until foamy, add sugar, beat until stiff. Spread on filling, sprinkle with coconut and brown lightly in medium oven.

Hon. Martha Bielish
The Senate
Alberta

Lemon Squares

1½ cups	rolled cracker crumbs	½ cup	white sugar
¾ cup	flour	1 cup	butter
½ cup	coconut	2 tbsp.	milk

Filling:

1 cup	water	1	egg
1 cup	sugar		juice and rind of 1 lemon
2 tbsp.	flour		

Combine first 4 ingredients. Mix butter into them and add milk. Put half the crumbs into 8" x 8" pan. Cook filling over medium heat until thickened, stirring constantly. Pour over crumb base. Put remaining crumbs on top. Bake in 350°F oven for 20-30 minutes.

Lowell Johnston, M.L.A.
Fifth Kings
Prince Edward Island

Lemon Squares

Base:

½ cup	butter	¾ tsp.	baking powder
½ cup	white sugar	½ tsp.	vanilla
1 cup	all-purpose flour	pinch	salt

Filling:

10 oz.	can (300 mL) Eagle Brand sweetened condensed milk		juice and rind of 2 lemons (save some rind for below)

Topping:

2	egg whites		a bit of the lemon rind
½ cup	sugar		

Combine base ingredients, pat into 9" x 9" pan and bake at 350°F until light brown, about 10-15 minutes. Do not overbake. Cool slightly and prepare filling. Beat sweetened condensed milk, add lemon juice and most of rind and beat again. Pour over base and spread evenly. Beat egg whites until foamy, beat in sugar gradually until soft peaks form. Fold in the bit of reserved lemon rind. Spread over filling. Bake at 350°F only until very lightly brown. If you like a thicker square you can use an 8" x 8" pan.

Hon. Lloyd MacPhail, M.L.A.
Second Queens
Prince Edward Island

Raisin Squares

Base:

1 cup	butter	1 tsp.	vanilla
¾ cup	white sugar	2 cups	flour
1	egg	2 tsp.	baking powder

Filling:

1½-2 cups	seeded raisins	2-3 tbsp.	flour
½ cup	white sugar	1 tbsp.	lemon juice
1 cup	boiling water		pinch salt

Cream butter and sugar. Add egg and vanilla and beat. Sift in dry ingredients. Cover 12" x 8" pan with half of base mixture. Cook filling ingredients until thick and pour over base. Put remainder of base mixture on top. Bake in 350°F oven 30-35 minutes.

Hon. Gerald Muirhead, M.L.A.
Arm River
Saskatchewan

Raisin Bars

Filling:

3¾ cups	raisins	1⅛ cups	orange juice
3 tbsp.	Rogers golden syrup	3 tbsp.	lemon juice
1½ tbsp.	cornstarch		grated rind of an orange

Crumb Mixture:

¾ cup	yellow sugar	½ tsp.	soda
1¾ cups	flour	1½ cups	rolled oats
½ tsp.	salt	¾ cup	butter OR margarine

Combine all filling ingredients, cook over medium heat, stirring, until thickened. Cover and cook over low heat another 5 minutes. Cool.

Measure dry ingredients for crumb mixture into bowl. Rub butter in until crumbly. Put ½ of crumbs in 9" x 12" pan. Spread with filling. Top with rest of crumbs.

Bake in 350°F oven for 30 minutes.

Nigel and Mary Pengelly
Nigel Pengelly, M.L.A.
Innisfail
Alberta

Date Squares

Filling:

1 lb.	dates	1 tsp.	vanilla
½ cup	brown sugar	pinch	salt
1 cup	water		

Crumb mixture:

1½ cups	brown sugar	½ tsp.	salt
1 cup	shortening	2 cups	flour
1 cup	rolled oats	1 tsp.	baking soda
1 tsp.	vanilla		

Bring filling ingredients to a boil. Cool. Prepare crumb mixture by crumbling all ingredients together. Pat half of mixture into 13" x 9" pan, spread on filling, then pat on rest of crumbs. Bake at 375°F for 25 minutes.

Peter B. MacLeod, M.L.A.
Third Kings
Prince Edward Island

Duncan Bars

This recipe takes 10 minutes to make. It is easy and tasty.

1	egg beaten	½ cup	walnuts OR almonds
1 tbsp.	cocoa	½ cup	coconut
¼ cup	brown sugar	1 tsp.	vanilla
½ cup	melted butter	2 tbsp.	melted semisweet chocolate
1½ cups	·graham wafer crumbs		

Combine first 8 ingredients and press into 8" x 8" pan. Spread on vanilla frosting of your choice. Melt 2 tbsp. of semisweet chocolate and swirl on top.

Brian and Dolores White
Brian K. White, M.P.
Dauphin - Swan River
Manitoba

Christmas Peppernuts (Pfeffernüsse)

This traditional Christmas cookie recipe has been in Gordon's family for at least 3 generations.

1½ cups	white sugar	1 tsp.	baking powder
2 cups	Roger's Golden Syrup	½ tsp.	each black pepper, ginger
¾ cup	milk		and cinnamon
¾ cup	lard	¼ tsp.	ginger
6 cups	white flour		

Combine syrup, sugar, milk and lard in a large saucepan. Heat on medium until lard is melted, stirring often. Do not boil. Cool to slightly warm.

Sift flour, baking powder and spices together. Add half of this to warm sugar mixture. Beat well. Add remainder and mix thoroughly.

Divide dough into 4 equal parts. Wrap in waxed paper or plastic and chill overnight.

Shape dough into a roll about 1" in diameter on a floured board. Cut roll into 1" cuts and place on greased cookie sheets.

Bake 8 minutes at 350°F, turn down to 325°F and bake 8 minutes longer or until a light golden brown but soft to the touch. Store in sealed containers.

Hon. Gordon Dirks, M.L.A.
Regina Rosemont
Saskatchewan

Pecan Crisps

This is a shortbread that our whole family loves!

1 cup	butter (do not substitute)	½ cup	flour
2 tsp.	vanilla	½ cup	cake flour
1 cup	icing sugar	3 oz.	chopped pecans

Beat first 3 ingredients with electric beaters until pale yellow colour. Mix in remaining ingredients. Spread in a greased jelly-roll pan, about 10" x 18". Keep the dough thicker on the edges where it cooks more quickly. Bake 15-18 minutes at 325-350°F depending on your oven. Cool, sprinkle with icing sugar and break into pieces.

Lorne and Fern Hepworth
Hon. Lorne Hepworth, M.L.A.
Weyburn
Saskatchewan

Raisin Drop Cookies

2 cups	brown sugar	1 tsp.	salt
¾ cup	shortening	2 tsp.	cinnamon
1 cup	milk	1 tsp.	nutmeg
2	eggs, beaten	1 tsp.	allspice
2½ cups	rolled oats	2 cups	raisins
1 tsp.	soda	2½ cups	flour

Cream sugar and shortening. Add remaining ingredients. Mix well and drop by teaspoonfuls onto buttered cookie sheet. Bake at 350°F for 15-20 minutes, until light brown.

Ernie and Sheila Isley
Hon. Ernie Isley, M.L.A.
Bonnyville
Alberta

Oatmeal Cookies

1 cup	butter	1 cup	white sugar
3 cups	oatmeal	½ tsp.	baking soda
1 cup	flour	2 tbsp.	milk
½ tsp.	salt		

Blend the first 5 ingredients like pastry. Add baking soda to milk. Pour over first mixture. Mix. Roll out and cut into circles. Bake at 350°F until brown.

Sometimes you may want to put 2 baked cookies together with jam or date filling.

Gay and John Caswell
Gay Caswell, M.L.A.
Saskatoon Westmount
Saskatchewan

Cowboy Cookies

1 cup	shortening	pinch	salt
1 cup	brown sugar	¾ tsp.	baking powder
1 cup	white sugar	2 cups	rolled oats
2	eggs	1 cup	chocolate chips
2 cups	flour	1 tsp.	vanilla

Cream shortening, brown and white sugars together well. Add eggs, mix well again. Add flour, salt and baking powder. Mix well. Add oats, chocolate chips and vanilla. Mix well again.

You will find this is a very heavy mixture and you may have to use your hands to blend in the final ingredients.

Drop by spoonfuls on cookie sheet and bake in a 350°F oven for about 10 to 12 minutes.

This makes approximately 5 dozen cookies so it will fill lots of little cowboys.

Hon. Alvin Hamilton, P.C., M.P.
Qu'Appelle-Moose Mountain
Saskatchewan

Peanut Butter Cookies

2 cups	flour (regular OR instant blending)	1 cup	peanut butter
		1 cup	granulated sugar
2 tsp.	soda	1 cup	brown sugar, packed
¼ tsp.	salt	2	eggs
1 cup	butter OR margarine		

Spoon or pour flour into dry measuring cup. Level off and pour onto waxed paper. Add soda and salt; stir well to blend.

Cream butter, peanut butter and sugars together thoroughly. Beat in eggs one at a time, mixing well after each addition. Add flour mixture to creamed mixture. Mix well.

Shape dough into 1" balls and place 2" apart on ungreased baking sheets. Press flat with floured fork. Bake at 375°F for 12-15 minutes. Yields about 6 dozen cookies.

Hon. Marvin Moore, M.L.A.
Smokey River
Alberta

Melting Moments

2 oz.	butter	2½ oz.	self-raising flour
1½ oz.	sugar		rolled oats OR coconut
½ tsp.	vanilla		glacé cherries

Cream butter and sugar, add vanilla. Stir flour in and mix thoroughly. Divide mixture into 12 pieces. Roll each into a ball with wet hands and coat with oats or coconut. Place on greased cookie sheet, press out slightly and place a small piece of cherry on centre of each cookie. Bake in a moderate oven, 325°F-350°F for 15-20 minutes.

Bev Harrison, M.L.A.
Saint John Fundy
New Brunswick

Raisin Thins

1 cup	butter	½ tsp.	baking soda
½ cup	brown sugar	¼ tsp.	salt
½ cup	white sugar	1 tsp.	vanilla
1	egg	½ cup	raisins
2 cups	flour		

Cream butter and sugar. Add well-beaten egg, flour sifted with soda and salt, vanilla and raisins. Shape into a roll, chill thoroughly. Slice ⅛" thick then bake quickly, in 375°F oven 7-10 minutes.

Hon. Leslie G. (Les) Young, M.L.A.
Edmonton Jasper Place
Alberta

Grands-péres du pays de l'érable

400 mL	de sirip d'érable		Une pincée de sel
300 mL	d'eau	50 mL	de beurre ou graisse
375 mL	de farine tout usage tamisée	200 mL	de lait
20 mL	de poudre à pâte		

Mélanger le sirop d'érable et l'eau. Amener à ébullition. Tamiser les ingrédients secs. Couper le gras jusqu'à ce que la préparation ressemble à une chapelure grossiére. Mélanger le lait pour obtenir une pâte molle. Déposer par mesures de 15 mL dans le mélange de sirop d'érable bouillant. Couvrir et mijoter 15 minutes sans lever le couvercle. Servir immédiatement.

Gilles and Doris Bernier
Gilles Bernier, M.P.
Beauce
Québec

Old-Fashioned Homemade Chocolates

3	eggs	5 x 1 oz.	squares unsweetened chocolate
¼ lb.	melted butter		
½ tsp.	salt	¼	bar paraffin wax
3 lbs.	icing sugar, approx.	4	bars Jersey Milk sweet chocolate bars

Beat eggs extremely well, add warm melted butter and salt; stir well. Slowly add sifted icing sugar. Add enough icing sugar to make dough smooth and unsticky, making sure that there are no lumps.

For different flavours, divide dough and add desired flavour to taste. Some popular flavours are vanilla, maple walnut, peppermint, licorice and cherry.

When adding the flavour, start with a small amount and mix it in thoroughly. More icing sugar is needed at this point.

If you want to make cherry chocolates you need a jar of maraschino cherries. You would then take a cherry and wrap it in cherry or vanilla-flavoured dough.

We roll the dough out with a rolling pin to about ⅝" thickness. We use different shapes for different flavours, these are cut with a knife or shaped by hand. The dough should now be chilled in preparation for dipping.

Chocolate for Dip:

Melt chocolate and wax in a double boiler. The chocolate should be put on to melt while dough is being mixed. It takes quite a while to melt.

Place a toothpick in the chilled, moulded filling and dip into the chocolate. After the chocolates have been dipped place on wax paper and chill to set. These chocolates freeze well and taste great!

Harry and Rose Baker
Harry Baker, M.L.A.
Biggar
Saskatchewan

Salzburger Nockerln

Since these come from Mozart's hometown, nockerln must be eaten while listening to Mozart.

3	eggs	1 tbsp.	flour, heaping
3 tbsp.	sugar	½ tbsp.	butter OR margarine
1 tsp.	vanilla		

Separate eggs and beat egg whites into a meringue. Stir in sugar and vanilla. Remove 3 tbsp. of the meringue and mix it into the lightly beaten yolks, then gently stir yolks into meringue. Sift flour over mixture and carefully fold in.

Melt butter in skillet. Using a tablespoon cut off 4 nockerln at a time from the meringue mixture, aiming for a triangular shape. Place them in the hot butter, fry until golden brown, turn and let them get just lightly browned on other side. Transfer to baking sheet and bake in preheated 350°F oven for 5 minutes. They must still be creamy inside — do not overbake. Dust with powdered sugar and serve at once. Serves 4.

Felix Holdmann, M.P.
Selkirk Interlake
Manitoba

Chocolate Balls

1 cup	peanut butter	2 cups	rice krispies
½ cup	butter	½ cup	walnuts
1 cup	icing sugar	6 oz.	pkg. chocolate chips
1 cup	coconut	½	slice Parawax

Combine first 3 ingredients and mix well. Add next 3 and mix well. Melt chocolate chips in a double boiler. Melt Parawax, stir into chocolate. Roll the first mixture into small balls and dip each 1 into the chocolate mixture.

Place on wax paper to cool. These can be frozen.

Hon. James M. Lee, P.C. M.L.A.
Premier of Prince Edward Island

Bud and Goldie's Fudge

2 cups	white sugar	1 cup	milk
2 cups	brown sugar	1 tsp.	vanilla
1 cup	butter	2 cups	flour, sifted
¼ cup	cocoa, optional		raisins OR walnuts

Bring sugars, butter, cocoa and milk to rolling boil, and boil for 10 minutes. Beat until stiff. Just before it starts to set add vanilla, flour and raisins or walnuts. Pour into a buttered pan.

Bud and Goldie Smith
A. L. (Bud) Smith, M.L.A.
Moose Jaw South
Saskatchewan

Sucre à la créme

1 tasse	de sucre blanc	3 c.	à table de sirop de mais
1 tasse	de cassonade	1 c.	à thé de vanille
1 tasse	de crème 35%		

Mélanger tous les ingrédients, faire fondre le tout à feu très doux (jusqu'à ce que le sucre soit fondu).

Amener à ébullition jusqu'à 212°F (boule molle dans l'eau froide). Une fois ce degré atteint, verser ce mélange dans une tôle graissée. Refroidir 5 minutes. Brasser jusqu'à épaississement du sucre à la crème.

Verser dans un moule 8"/8" graissé. Mettre dans le réfrigérateur durant une heure avant de servir.

NOTE: Si désiré ajouter les noix lorsque vous verser dans la tôle.

Pierre H. Vincent, M.P.
Trois-Rivières
Québec

Recipe Index

Donor Index

The Blue Book of Canadian Cuisine

Please send me _____ copies of "The Blue Book of Canadian Cuisine" at $12.95 per book plus $1.50 (total order) for mailing.

Enclosed is $_____.

Name: _____

Street: _____

City: _____ Province (State) _____

Postal Code (Zip Code) _____

Please make cheques or money order payable to:
   Annaperce Holdings Ltd.
   Box 606
   Melfort, Saskatchewan
   Canada   S0E 1A0

Price is subject to change.

Treat Your Friends to

The Blue Book of Canadian Cuisine

Please send me _____ copies of "The Blue Book of Canadian Cuisine" at $12.95 per book plus $1.50 (total order) for mailing.

Enclosed is $_____.

Name: _____

Street: _____

City: _____ Province (State) _____

Postal Code (Zip Code) _____

Please make cheques or money order payable to:
   Annaperce Holdings Ltd.
   Box 606
   Melfort, Saskatchewan
   Canada   S0E 1A0

Price is subject to change.